From the Class of Dudes
to the
Class of Legends in Christ

Gbenga Oduniyi

PublishAmerica
Baltimore

Unless otherwise indicated, all scripture quotations are taken from the King James Version of the Holy Bible.

Scripture quotations marked NIV are taken from New International Version of the Holy Bible Copyright c 1978, 1984 International Bible Society.

Scripture quotations marked Amplified are taken from Amplified Version of the Holy Bible.

First printing

At the specific preference of the author, PublishAmerica allowed this work to remain exactly as the author intended, verbatim, without editorial input.

ISBN: 1-4137-9791-1
PUBLISHED BY PUBLISHAMERICA, LLLP
www.publishamerica.com
Baltimore

From the Class of Babes to the Class of Legends in Christ

Gbenga Oduniyi

To: The Very Revd (Dr) Adams/

I had the honour of launching
this book in Vienna.

With Compliments

from: The Very Brother 'Yinka Okuwoga.

12th August 2006.

TABLE OF CONTENT

FOREWORD

As I read this book, I cannot but share with other readers the conviction in my spirit man that God has given Brother Gbenga Oduniyi the gift of discernment, revelation knowledge, as well as an insight into His thoughts to mankind in writing this book. This book is a rare treasure of Godly wisdom to mankind through an anointed vessel of His, to remind every believer of His expectations for our lives upon salvation of our souls.

This is not just any book. It shows how off the mark many believers are. Many Christians appear to have lost the focus of the Lord's expectations for their lives, they have become complacent and nonchalant to the work of our Lord, their personal relationships with the Lord has become casual, it is thus high time to wake out of spiritual sleep and slumber.

The inspiration given to Brother Gbenga Oduniyi to write this book is a reflection of the loving movement of God towards the people He has made and wishes to rescue from spiritual decay and mediocrity by elevating them to the level of a spiritual Legend. The writing of the book could not have been anything, but inspired by the

Holy Spirit as the information being passed on to whosoever desires to do exploits for the Lord has been based on the scripture.

This book will also revolutionize, energize and revitalize every reader. As a believer, if you want: to be not just a passive Christian, to dream great dreams, achieve the best results for the Lord, then this is a "must-read" book for you, it is an invaluable aid for personal spiritual Legend. As you read this book, I pray you will rise up to the challenge.

Pastor Folajimi TAIWO
Parish Pastor
The Redeemed Christian Church of God (RCCG)
Chapel of His Glory Parish
Vienna, Austria, August 2005.

Introduction

The dictionary meaning of the word "legend" simply means famous person. And the word "famous" means very well known, excellent, while the word "excellent" means to be outstandingly good at something, very good. Of course you know that among the children of God there are some that are famous, who are outstandingly good in their ministries. Though all are children, still while some are salient, famous and well known, some others are silent, unnoticed. Yet, they are all children of God! If we are to mention the names of the twelve apostles of Jesus off hands, some names can easily and quickly be mentioned, because they are famous. However, for us to mention the names of other apostles we need to really think because their names don't ring the bell. What makes a man famous if not for what he does and achieve. The Bible gives us the record of many legends, not only that, it tells us what to do in other to become a legend and vice versa.

The Church is the gathering of the legends. No one born-again is born a slave. No one born-again is born slave. Every genuinely born-again Christian is a born legend, but not all manifest as legend. All the children of God are given the grace to become famous in the army of God, however not all manifest. What makes some to manifest and others not to, as well as what we need to do in other to manifest what God has made us to be is part of what we shall consider together in this book. Christianity is more than having cars, building houses, having children and all the rest. The call of God upon our lives and our destiny in Christ Jesus as children of the Most High God is more than what many people spend all their life-time asking for, while they fail to realize what God has called them to be in life. The day you discover God's purpose for your life, that very day will mark the day you will begin to enjoy the full support of heaven, when you will live stress-free, sorrow-free, burden-free life. Pastors and evangelists are not the only ones called to be legends. Every member of the body of Christ is born to be famous. All the children of God are born great.

Some salient and silent people in Bible days

The Bible is a story about legends. It is important to know that the Bible never talks about men in multitudes, but of men and women who stood out, individuals who affect lives, nations and the entire human race by their actions or inactions. Right from the first and to the last books of the Bible, God reveals so many legends to us. Due to time and space, we shall consider only a very few of them. Now, being a legend is not limited to having anointing to heal the sick and raise the dead. Being a legend in the army of the Lord is more and goes beyond this. It all depends on the calling of the Lord upon your life. Just as no part of the body is created to be useless, neither is any was made to be inferior or less important, so is every one of us Christians, who are parts of the body of Christ. Only the idle, the fearful and the lazy ones would change their glory to shame, but one thing is certain, once you are born again you are born great, you are born legend.

The first person whose life thrilled me in the Bible is the first ever known friend of God. Before I mention his name, I want to remind us of someone here. When the Bible was mentioning the names of the great men in the government of David, the Bible made mention of one person who ordinarily you would not consider necessary. Not only that, while they were mentioned according to their importance and rank, the list started from the least to the greatest, this man's name was mentioned next to the highest man, the commander of the royal army. That was Hushai. The Bible says he was the friend of the king. That was his job, yet he occupied a higher position than Jonathan, David's uncle who was a counsellor, a man of insight and a scribe. He was higher than Ahithophel the top among the king's counsellors. Hushai was the friend of the king, and that made him famous among the top members of David's cabinet. That was with David, the man after the heart of God. Let us now consider the first ever known best friend of God.

At the age of 65 Enoch discovered something in life that made him a legend. While other people who lived before him and during his life time were forgotten and were cut off from the Lord, Enoch chose to walk with God. He walked with God for 300 years. God was so pleased with Enoch that God took him away. I believe God considered Enoch as a man that was important to Him than allow him to spend some time in hade, in the grave. If Enoch had died, he would have remained in the grave till now. But because his friendship was so precious to God, God could not afford to lose his friendship; therefore, God took him away to be with God for ever. Abraham died, and was buried, but Enoch didn't die, he lives on with God. That's a legend, famous among the people of God.

Just as science and technology is so wide such that if you are gifted you still have opportunity to make name, so it is in the body of Christ. The quality of Enoch's walk with the Lord made him a legend. You can be an intercessor or a prayer warrior and still become a legend of the Lord. It is not only the gifts we use in the presence of the congregation that make us famous, what we do at times behind the scene is still enough to make us famous. It is reported that the Pastor of one of the largest churches in the world which has close to a million congregation once said that the head of the prayer warrior of the church is a woman. She must be a mighty prayer warrior you will agree. While the Pastor of the Church is honoured and well known, this woman too is famous whenever the church is being mentioned.

No matter your gift, it is enough to bring you to fame. I dare to say this, of these three – faith, hope and love, the greatest of them all is love. Of all the spiritual gifts, the greatest of them all is love. May I say this, when genuine love is what prompts your actions, greatness will be the next story that will be said about you. The Bible says that because God loved the world, He gave Jesus to the world. Christ Jesus also died on the cross because of the love He had for mankind. In fact, His death on the cross was a down payment that any man who must see the glory, power and the kingdom of God must first accept this love of God and of Christ. And, to accept this love is to accept Jesus as your Lord and personal Saviour. The Bibles says that among faith, hope and love, the greatest is love. The key to greatness is not really in the amount of your fasting and prayer. Rather it is when you first receive the love of God and then you show the same love to both God and man. Thus, when the exercise of your gift comes out of love, compassion on the recipient of your action, you will certainly receive the support of heaven. It is important that we mention here that the first spiritual gift you were given when you come to God was love. God gave you and me the greatest of all the gifts. Put in another way, the first gift God gave us was the greatest gift and He did this that we might become legends, famous people in the kingdom of God. Hence, the type of gift that you have is not what makes you great in the kingdom of God, rather exercising those gifts out of love. Take for instance, what was the gift Joseph had that brought him to the palace, that was powerful enough to wipe out his "crime" which brought him into prison and made a foreigner to become the governor of the then the only super-power nation of the world? It was the gift to dream and interpret dreams. Was it the well-celebrated gift that made Daniel great in his days that made a slave to become so great in Babylon? No, it was just the ability to ask and receive answer from God, and the gift to receive revelation from God. Your gift surely has the potential to bring you into the class of the legends.

After the departure of Enoch, one would have thought that his first son Methuselah would follow the footstep of his father. In fact,

I believe God gave Methuselah more years to live than any other man that ever lived on earth just to appreciate the walk of his father with the Lord. But, the man Methuselah lived an empty life, he lived the longest but did nothing with the opportunity he had. He had all the opportunity to be a legend, to build on from where his father stopped. But that is not it. Thus among the famous people in the Bible, Methuselah is not to be found.

If I may ask, what made Abraham famous? His faith in God is the answer. At a time when there was no record of God's act. At a time when there was no Bible, when there was no record of the acts of God, Abraham believed the Lord for a child even at his old age. Not only that, he moved away from his father's house, and his nation to follow the Lord God he probably had heard nothing about. He received the promise after 25 years still his faith did not fail. And considering all he went through, coupled with his faith, he became famous among the people of God. He is the first citizen that received the saints of the Lord into his bosom after death. Adam was not counted worthy to receive the saints into his bosom, not even Noah the first man to receive the grace of God was able to win this enviable position, only Abraham, and he became the father of faith. In fact, he became the human father of the people of God, while Adam remains the father of the sinful men. Thus Abraham became famous, or rather a legend because of the faith he demonstrated.

Joshua was someone that became a legend through dedication. He was the personal assistant of Moses. But he was dedicated. And God took notice of that. I believe he was just dedicated to duty without any ambition of being Moses' replacement. If he were to be ambitious, first God might not have chosen him and secondly, he would not have been unwilling to take the position, or fearful of the challenges before him, which God saw in him that made God to say to him severally "Fear not,…be courageous…I am with you just as I was with Moses" In the wilderness, each time God wanted Moses to come to the mountain for a meeting, while He would command Moses not to allow any other person or elder of the Israelites to approach the mountain, Moses had the privilege to go beyond where the elders could reach. Apart from this, there was a Tent of Meeting where Moses usually met with God. Only Moses could enter the Tent, even Aaron the high priest could not. Whenever Moses went out to the Tent, all the Israelites would stand at the entrance of their own tents. Each time Moses entered the Tent, pillar of cloud would stand at the entrance of the Tent, to signify "Road Block". After his meeting with the Lord, the Bible has this to say;

"Then Moses would return to the camp, but his young aide Joshua son of Nun did not leave the Tent" (Exodus 33:11)

He was dedicated to serving his master. He had the interest of his master at heart. He was a man that believed in the power and the faithfulness of God, after all, he never left the Presence of the Lord. While Moses was coming into and going out of the Tent (the Presence of God) Joshua was soaking himself in the presence of the Lord. When God would now pick a replacement for Moses, though the children of Aaron were to succeed their father, but that was not the same with Moses. God picked Joshua and gave him all the encouragement that he needed to occupy that enviable position. Thus, Joshua became a legend by being dedicated to serving his master Moses. These days when everyone thinks that establishing a church and being called Bishop, Pastor, Founder and General Overseer is the gateway to being prominent and famous in the body of Christ, I tell you, even as you serve your pastor diligently, with all your heart, doing it from your heart by supporting your pastor to achieve the vision God gave him, you can still be a legend.

Rehab who was formerly a prostitute shot her way to become famous among the people of God simply by making herself available for the use of the Lord. The spies needed protection, she was willing to offer that for them. Not only that, she believed in their God given vision even when many of the Israelites in the wilderness could not believe that vision, Rehab did. She hid the Israeli spies, plugged herself in into the vision by telling them to spare her and her relations when Israel eventually conquered Jericho. She was spared, and later she got married to Salmon and became the mother of Boaz, thus she became the great grand mother of David and Jesus. Though the

14

tradition of the Jews forbids mentioning and counting the women, still, when the record of the Christ was being given in the New Testament, Rahab was mentioned and when the Bible presented the faith hall of fame in Hebrews Chapter 11, Rahab, though she was once a Gentile and a prostitute, her name was mentioned. That simply means, you can be among the people who are written off from being great in the sight of the Lord. You might lack gifts and anointing now. It may even be that you are very new in the faith. These conditions are not enough to disqualify you from becoming a legend. Making yourself available for the use of the Lord is enough to make you famous and great.

I once heard of a man who on his own went into an agreement with the Lord on the issue of his tithe. He told God that rather than giving God ten percent of his income while he takes ninety percent; he would prefer to reverse it. He would give God ninety percent of his income while he would spend only ten percent! When many of us struggle to give ten percent willingly, he was willing to give God ninety percent. By that decision, he became a financial legend in the Lord as the Lord prospered him so much in his business that he became a financial giant that sponsors great number of evangelical programmes. When the Lord blessed His people by saying that you shall be the head and not the tail, you shall be above only. God was simply saying that at the top there is enough room to accommodate all of us. If for any reason you do not come to "the above" it is not as if someone else will occupy your place, that place will be vacant, for there is more than enough room and space for us all.

Since we are not part of the silent people, we shall not dwell much about this group. Methuselah was among the prominent people in this class. He lived 969 years without any achievement. Jesus lived for 33 years, yet He is the most discussed person in the history of the world. He is the one person about whom the highest number of books has been written. Yet Jesus only lived three percent of the life Methuselah lived. Just three percent! Did someone say that was Jesus? David lived just seven percent of the number of the life of Methuselah, Methuselah is lost in history. He is remembered only for living long empty life.For John the Baptist, the angel that brought the news of his birth clearly said that John the Baptist would be great in the sight of the Lord. He was filled with the Holy Spirit right from his mother's womb. The anointing upon him was so powerful to the extent that, even though he had his church in the wilderness, great number of people went to him to hear the gospel, and they repented of their sins and were baptized. And Jesus gave this testimony that among the people that lived in the Old Testament days, even from Adam to John the Baptist, there was no one as great as John. This also means that John was greater than Elijah, Abraham, Noah, Moses, David and others. But Jesus added this, "The least in the kingdom of God", that is, the least person under the New Testament dispensation "is greater than John the Baptist". What a revelation Jesus gave us. What a great and effectual door to greatness and fame God has opened before every one of us that gives his or her life to Jesus! I tell you, this is awesome. Every Christian is greater in status than the man reported to be the greatest man in the Old Testament dispensation. If a Christian died wretched, it is not because God made his life so, rather, he died wretched because of ignorance.

Chapter One
The needs for new legends

"...He requested for himself that he might die, and said, It is enough: now O Lord, take away my life." In every generation, God has some legends in the body of Christ, the anointed men and women of God that have fire of the Holy Ghost burning in their bones. They derive joy in doing the will of the Lord, even if it means losing their own lives for they are determined to fulfil the purpose of the Lord concerning their lives. They are all around us today, famous in the body of Christ. They are very few but, they are powerful movers of the hands of God. They hate to see souls perishing in sins, therefore, they cry unto the Lord for anointing, no matter the amount of anointing they have, they still pray for more. That is why we see great men and women of God who have great anointing, yet desire for more. When they go on their kneels before the Father, they see themselves as little children that need the help of the Father more than ever before. As they receive increasing anointing, of course it is never for their own benefit, but to profit the Church. The book of

Isaiah Chapter Sixty-One reveals to us that the anointing upon the man of God is given him to profit the Church, the body of Christ, as he ministers to the meek, the broken-hearted, the captives and to those imprisoned by the devil. When they are anointed to heal for instance, it is not as if they will be healing themselves, rather they are given the gifts to profit the Church. Think of the man of God blessed with the gift of working miracles such as raising the dead, that gift is not given him so that he would die and raise himself up. Rather, the gift is given him to be a blessing in the Church, the body of Christ.

The legends are not happy to see people suffering under the oppression of the devil, more so, when they know that it is possible (through Christ Jesus) for these people to enjoy freedom and peace. They therefore derive joy in destroying the works of the devil every where they go. They are eager to preach the gospel to the lost souls. They thereby depict hell to expand the kingdom of God. They love to demonstrate the power of the Living God and as they do that they bring glory to God. With them in the army of God, the heaven is happy, for there is hardly a day that they do not make the angels of God to rejoice.

"Likewise, I say unto you, there is joy in the presence of the angels of God over one sinner that repenteth" (Luke 15:10)

Again, Jesus said;

"I say unto you, that likewise joy shall be in heaven over one sinner that repenteth"

(Luke 15:7)

When a single soul repents, there is joy in heaven in the presence of the angels of God. Now, if the whole angels of God in heaven will rejoice over just a single soul that repents, what then will happen when tens, hundreds or thousands of souls repent at a single meeting or crusade? There shall be an explosion of joy. The angels of God will repeatedly appreciate the death and the resurrection of Jesus Christ. Great joy will erupt in heaven. The reason the legends do not joke with evangelism is that they know that in it lies the power of God to save mankind. To the legends, the best gift you can give to man is extending to him the gift of salvation which is the love of God.

The legends are never satisfied even when the size of the congregation of their church is the largest in the whole world. They still pray to the Lord of harvest to give them grace to win more souls to the kingdom of God, for they know that there is at least someone in the village, town, city, country and in the world that is not yet born-again. Irrespective of their present achievement, they still want to achieve more. They are terrors to the kingdom of darkness, for their manifestation brings destruction to the works of the devil. They go to the battles, fight and win without being wounded. The devil knows them, in hell they are well known, respected and feared. Whenever and wherever demons see them, they know that there is an abrupt end to evil activities, for these legends will cast them out.

Like we discussed in the introductory part of this book, the gift you have does not really matter. You can be a seasoned Church administrator and still be a legend, an administrator that made it impossible for the devil to creep in into the Church. You can be a prayer warrior and still be a legend—a prayer warrior that causes confusion and destruction in the camp of the enemy of God. You can be an usher in the Church and still be a legend. An usher is an official who receives and leads people to their seats, as in the Church. When a human agent sent from the pit of hell to implement evil plan in the Church gets to where you are, as you minister to him, and he sees you (because you are like a fiery giant before them) the fire of the Holy Ghost must consume him and his plan destroyed. The forces of darkness will soon be afraid of you and would prefer coming to Church services only when you are not there to minister. I am saying this so that as you read this book, in your mind you will not be thinking that only the preachers of the word are called to be legends. No. In fact, you can be a Church cleaner and still be a legend. You can clean the seats and decree that anyone that shall sit on them shall be met by the Lord. When the unsaved sit here they shall be saved. When the sick sit on these seats they shall be healed. Through that, you and not the pastor that stands to preach may be the one causing miracles of salvation and healing to happen. Of course, people may not know, but God knows, the holy angels know and the forces of hell also know this truth. That is some of the roles the legends play in the Church.

Great is the worth of these legends in the sight of the Lord. They are precious temple of the Holy Ghost, the altar of the Lord which is their heart, offerings and sacrifices never cease. God is proud of them and protects them jealously. For the fact that they are the carriers of the Holy Ghost, whenever enemies will arise against them, the Holy Ghost Himself will arise to fight the battle.

"So shall they fear the name of the LORD from the west, and His glory from the rising of the sun. When the enemy shall come in like a flood, the Spirit of the Lord shall lift up a standard against him" (Isaiah 59:19)

Since they carry the anointing of the Lord, the Lord keeps watch over them and places a placard on them.

"Saying, touch not mine anointed, and do my prophets no harm" (Psalm 105:15)

Legends too are mortal

The legends, people famous in the army of God are around us, they are planted in every nation of the world. But, the legends will not live in the world, doing the work of the Lord forever.

"And as it is appointed unto men once to die, but after this the judgment" (Hebrews 9:27)

One day, one after the other, all the legends in a generation will die. Yet, the church of Christ must live on. Yes, the legends will one day depart from the church, far away from the world, but the Lord Jesus that redeemed man through His precious blood lives on for ever more. Though these legends, the generals in the Lord's army sleep in the Lord, Jesus the head of the Church never sleeps nor slumbers. The legends would die, however, the Giver of the anointing the Holy Ghost remains alive and active in the Church.

Surely, God knows the date of departure of every legend in the Church. He will not leave His Church desolate, hence, the need for replacement. In every Church, every denomination, in every nation of the world, the Lord searches for men and women that will be appointed to replace the legends. The Lord will raise men of valour that will continue the work of the ministry left behind by the legends. However, our Eternal Lord does not wait till the legends pass away before He begins the search. Rather, while the legends are still alive, the replacements would be prepared, trained for the work to be committed to their hands, such that no vacuum is created in the Christendom.

Forgetting the first love

"Nevertheless, I have somewhat against thee, because thou hast left thy first love. Remember therefore from whence thou art fallen, and repent, and do the first works; or else I will come unto thee quickly, and will remove thy candlestick out of his place, except thou repent"* (Revelation 2:4-5)

Death is not the only thing that calls for the replacement of the legends. Self-fulfilment makes some men of God to forget their first love. Until now, they were zealous, organising many outreach programmes, crusades, in cities and villages. But now that they have a name and are rich, they tend to relax, and forget their first love.

"I know thy works, and thy labour, and thy patience, and how thou canst not bear them which are evil: and thou hast tried them which say they are apostles, and are not, and hast found them liars" (Revelation 2:2)

It is not as if the legends that fall into this category have stopped working for the Lord. They are very much in active service.

"And hast borne, and hast patience, and for my name's sake hast laboured, and hast not fainted" (Revelation 2:3)

Such legends are still preaching the gospel, but not as effective as in the time past. Perhaps in the time past they preached on radio, television and organised crusades, but now, they have limited the soul-winning to the four corners of their churches. In the time past, the legends would fast and pray fervently before going to the pulpits, but now, going to the pulpits is a routine, without passion or definite purpose, they preach because they must preach. When they started the Church, they greatly searched for souls; they had a fantastic follow-up strategy for the visitors to their Church programmes. However, now they believe the Lord will bring people into the

Church even when they make little or no effort. Except such legends repent, the Lord will come *quickly* to do one thing, to remove their candlestick. Let us see what the candlestick stand for.

"The mystery of the seven stars which thou sawest in my right hand, and the seven golden candlesticks. The seven stars are the angels of the seven churches: and the seven candlesticks which thou sawest are the seven churches." Revelation 1:20

The Lord said to the church of Ephesus; I will come quickly and remove your candlestick. Yet, the candlestick stands for the Church. The *real Church* is the candlestick that will be removed from the Church. The removal of the candlestick is the departure of the glory of God from the Church. The Church will continue to exist for just one reason, because of the word of the Lord that says the gates of hell shall not prevail over the Church. The glory of the Lord has departed from many Churches today. The Lord has removed the *real Church* from the Church, such that the Church is void of the seal and approval of God, until a leader will arise in such a Church that will bring back the lost glory of God, the story will be the same.

When the legends think that they are fulfilled, and need nothing more, the Lord will raise some other people to replace them. As a result, many legends though they are still living, they have been replaced. Many Churches that were great some decades ago have been replaced by new ones, thus they become the synagogue of the Jews where they meet to read the laws, that is, the Scriptures but rejected Christ the real word of God.

The need to replace Elijah

When Moses finished his assignment, Joshua took over from him. When King Saul was rejected by the Lord, during his life time, David was anointed. The Lord will not for any reason allow the work of the ministry to be grounded. During His three years in the ministry, the Lord made frantic efforts to ensure that when He shall return to the Father, the world would not miss Him, nor will there be a vacuum. For His departure to be a great blessing to the world, He taught His disciples and also gave them power and authority. Though, for about three years He taught His disciples about the

Kingdom of God, for forty days after His resurrection from the dead, He still taught them about the same kingdom of God.

"To whom also He shewed Himself alive after His passion by many infallible proofs, being seen of them forty days, and speaking of the things pertaining to the kingdom of God." Acts 1:3

Jesus ensured that they believed in Him, He equipped them with the word of God that they might become better and multiple replacements. On the day of Pentecost, the Lord perfected the work of preparing the disciples when He baptised them all with the Holy Ghost and fire.

Prophet Elijah was a great man of God, a legend and a general in the army of the Lord. He was ever ready and willing to prove that the Lord is God. Of course his name Eli-Jah means the Lord is God. He predicted a famine in Israel and affirmed that rain should not fall except by his word. He assembled and defeated the prophets of Baal in a contest he arranged on Mount Carmel. He seemed to find it easy to call down fire from heaven. He did not taste death, in whirlwind of horses and fire, he was taken to heaven. Later, he appeared in glory with Moses at the transfiguration of Jesus (Mark 9:1-8)

Though he was great, the threat of Queen Jezebel made Elijah run for his dear life. Elijah seemed to be fed up. It was as if the Israelites could not be reconciled back to God. He had just proved to the people on Mount Carmel that Jehovah is God, now the queen was calling for his head.

Record outside the Bible has it that Jezebel's father was the high priest in a pagan temple in Tyre. However, he murdered the king of Tyre, and ruled in that nation for about thirty-two years! His reign was characterized by murderous idolatries and a reckless contempt for human rights. Ahab, the king of Israel had married Jezebel as a political strategy to ensuring peace with the nation of Tyre. Being a true daughter of her evil father, Jezebel installed hundreds of prophets of Baal, and ordered the wholesale slaughter of prophets of God that opposed her. With the knowledge of the personalities of Jezebel and her father, the threat of Jezebel made Elijah run for his dear life. He was fed up, frustrated, tired of the work of the ministry and therefore asked God for retirement.

"*...He requested for himself that he might die, and said, It is enough: now O Lord, take away my Life*".

Elijah pleaded with the Lord that his appointment be terminated, he wanted to quit. But God was not going to beg him. When a man tells God, "It is enough" The Lord will not say "Continue" In the work of the ministry, when a man puts full-stop sign to his statement before the Lord, God is not going to say anything thereafter.

Are you tired of your present work of the ministry? Are you fed up, such that you think quitting is the only way out? Wait upon the Lord for your strength to be renewed. Do not quit, stay on. Pray for the grace to remain in service. Every legend has an appointed time to withdraw, do not withdraw before your appointed time. Of course, the agents of the devil in the Church will arise to discourage and frustrate you, yet you must stand your ground. It is even possible that the so called elders of the Church are the ones the devil is using to frustrate you. The elders of the Church may be people who have no knowledge and no vision but would still want to show you how to work in the vineyard of the Lord. I tell you this truth, it is better you leave such a Church than quit the ministry the Lord has committed into your hand. Jesus once told His disciples when He sent them out to preach the gospel; saying which ever city they entered and they were not accepted or welcome, the disciples should leave such a city and go to another city. Some Christians have allowed some agents of the evil one in the church to discourage them from continuing in the ministry committed to them by the Lord. I believe it is better to leave such a congregation than to fail to fulfil the work of the ministry, simply because, on the day of reckoning, God is going to hold you responsible for the decision you have taken. No excuse for failure will be entertained.

Once you are determined to do the will of the Lord, you can always count on the support of the Lord. No matter the plan of the evil one against you, you are already marked for victory.

"*Ye are of God, little children, and have overcome them: because greater is He that is in you, than he that is in the world*" 1 John 4:4

As a legend, a great man in the sight of the Lord, Elijah would not be replaced by a single man. Hear what the Lord told Elijah;

"... Go, return on thy way to the wilderness of Damascus: and when thou comest, anoint Hazael to be king over Syria:

And Jehu the son of Nimshi shalt thou anoint to be King over Israel: and Elisha the son of Shaphat of Abelmeholah shalt thou anoint to be prophet in thy room" (1 Kings 19:15 &16)

Why would God instruct Elijah to anoint two Kings and a prophet?

"And it shall come to pass, that him that escapeth the sword of Hazael (the king of Syria) *shall Jehu* (the king of Israel) *slay: and him that escapeth from the sword of Jehu shall Elisha* (the prophet) *slay"* (1 Kings 19:17)

When the Lord takes away a legend, He replaces him with more than one person. His reason for this is for the purpose of progress. When Jesus departed, He left behind eleven apostles and many disciples. About one hundred and twenty disciples received the Holy Ghost on the day of Pentecost.

Chapter Two
God is not partial

"And the Lord said unto him, Go, return on thy way to the wilderness of Damascus: and when thou comest, anoint Hazael to be the king over Syria: And Jehu the son of Nimshi shalt thou anoint to be the king over Israel: and Elisha the son of Shaphat of Abelmeholah shalt thou anoint to be prophet in thy room" (1 Kings 19:15 & 16)

While Elijah tabled his letter of resignation before God, the Lord went through the nation of Israel searching for a best replacement. In the nation of Israel at that time, even though Jezebel had set out to wipe out the worship of the true God by wholesale killing of the prophets of God, there were still many prophets of God in the land of Israel.

God has many choices

When Elijah instructed Obadiah the servant of Ahab to inform Ahab that Elijah was around, Obadiah seized that opportunity to tell Elijah one good and godly thing he had secretly done.

"Was it not told my lord what I did when jezebel slew the prophets of the Lord, how I hid an hundred men of the Lord's prophets by fifty in a cave, and fed them with bread and water?" (1 Kings 18:13)

Now, these words of Obadiah revealed that there were a hundred prophets of the Lord kept and preserved by this servant of King Ahab. Apart from this, when Elijah was shouting and making a claim before the Lord saying that he was the only prophet of God left in the nation of Israel, and complained that they were seeking to kill him. Then, the Lord replied him saying;

"Yet I have left me seven thousand in Israel, all the kneels which have not bowed unto baal, and every mouth which hath not kissed him" (1 Kings 19:18)

The New Testament has this record;

"God has not cast away His poeple which He foreknew. Wot ye not what the scripture saith of Elias? how he maketh intercession to God against Israel, saying; Lord, they have killed your prophets, and digged down your altars; and I am left alone, and they seek my life. But what saith the answer of God unto him? I have reserved to myself seven thousand men, who have not bowed the knee to the image of Baal" (Romans 11:2-4)

Apart from the hundred prophets of the Lord kept by Obadiah, and the seven thousand preserved by the Lord, it is important that we know that Elijah hitherto had a servant. Before he resigned his appointment with God he had a servant that could be referred to as a prophet in training, the Old Testament books usually referred to them as the sons of the prophets. All this while, there was a young man that had been serving Elijah. But Elijah left him at Beersheba (1 Kings 19:39). Of all these people God had to choose just one person to serve as a prophet in the place of Elijah. Now, God had at least seven thousand one hundred and one people from whom He needed to choose one person.

One would have expected that the right person to be anointed to replace Elijah was his servant, the man who had been serving Elijah all this while. But the Bible stated that he left this servant at Beersheba. God is not denominational, if He will raise someone to replace a great man of God in a particular Church; He is not compelled to pick a man from that same Church. His divine aim is to raise a man that will perform the same duty not necessarily in that church, but in the Christendom at large.

We would have thought that God would consider someone among the sons of the prophets, but God is neither tribalism nor racial. He can be pleased to raise a black man to replace a white evangelist. Man may see differences among various men, nations and colour, but God sees us as members of the same family. We could have also expected God to appoint one of the sons of the prophets in Second Kings Chapter Two, men that could see clearly into the future, they that knew before hand the precise day Elijah would be taken away. They could see vision clearly; they were indeed prophets in training. "One of them should at least qualify" one would think. But God does not look out for the mighty and the strong to do mighty works, rather, He loves to use the feeble, the weak, who humble and submit themselves for the use of the Lord that He alone might receive glory when great works are accomplished.

Thus, God refused to appoint the servant of Elijah, He would not even appoint any of the hundred fearful prophets of God kept by the servant of the king who fled to save their lives from been killed by Jezebel. Neither would God allow Elijah to anoint any of the seven thousand people. Yet, He would not pick a person from the highly gifted prophets in training, called the sons of the prophets.

Surprisingly, God chose Elisha, a young man that had little or no experience in prophet-hood ministry. He was a farmer, a full time, big time mechanized farmer. For God to have neglected all the "potential prophets" while He chose a farmer, then, there must be something that God kept searching for among all the children of Israel which could not be found even among the sons of the prophets, except in a farmer.

When the Lord was fed up with King Saul, He carried out a search throughout the land of Israel. While the Lord was making the search, He had in His mind an attribute He was looking out for in the life of every man that may occupy the throne. Replacement was necessary because the Lord could no longer bear with Saul. Even when Samuel kept interceding for Saul, the Lord told him to stop the intercessory prayer, since He had rejected Saul from reigning over Israel (1 Samuel 16:1)

The Lord had begun a search for replacement; therefore, He would not want to be stopped by the prayer of His beloved servant Samuel. He rejected Saul by removing him from His presence from being the king of Israel.

"And when He had removed him, He raised up unto them David to be their king: to whom also He gave testimony, and said, I have found David the son of Jesse, a man after mine own heart, which shalt fulfil all my will." Acts 13:22.

Finding is the result and the fruit produced by search. The Lord searched round and found David, a man after God's heart that would fulfil ALL His will. The Lord was not searching for a handsome man to reign over His people Israel. He was not compelled to pick Prince Jonathan the son of Saul as replacement. We know that Jonathan loved David and was a man of faith, remember he once said this word of faith during a war time when he said to his armour-bearer; "…For there is no restraint to the Lord to save by many or by few" (1 Samuel 14:6) However, faith is not the only requirement needed by a man to get qualified to replace the legend. To choose a replacement for Saul, God also had no delight in any of the men of war that were strong in battle. God only wanted a man that had the heart of God, that is to say, a man that had a heart for the things of God. Not a self-centred or selfish man that will only cater for his pocket and household, but a godly man ever willing to do the will of God. He searched for the man that would fulfil God's will for the people of that generation. Not a man that would fulfil half of God's will but fulfil *all* His will. Likewise, to replace Elijah, God wanted a man that would fulfil all His will concerning the people of that generation. He wanted a man that was not just interested in power but also in fulfilling all the will of God.

There are many great and mighty men of God in all the six continents of the world. Think of evangelists that gather great multitudes and win thousands of souls to the kingdom of God in just a single meeting. Consider the servants of the Lord greatly blessed with overflowing anointing, who through the power of the Holy Spirit heal great number of sicknesses which medical doctors had certified incurable. Just imagine the men and the women of God so greatly endowed to teach the word in a simple form and it's as if you had not heard or read the word before, you are so touched that the impact of the word in your life is great and permanent. Consider also the servants of the Lord flowing in the anointing of the Lord through prophetic utterances calling what is not as if they are, and thus bringing them to be. As demons knew and confessed that they knew Jesus and Paul, they also know these legends. Every where these legends go, demons are demoralized, they are in great confusion and everlasting shame. Think about the anointed servants of God who write articles and books with "pens of fire", what spoken word can do, their writings perform the same.

However, one thing is sure, as the second coming of the Lord tarries, these legends will not live forever on earth, hence, the Lord is searching for people that will replace them. He will however not anoint wrong people except they that will fulfil all His will. If until now you are far from the will of the Lord, unless you repent you cannot be a replacement for any of these legends. If what you enjoy doing is that which stands contrary to the will of the Lord, unless you repent, you have just disqualified yourself by the reason of your action. You can only replace an ordinary member of the congregation, even people like Ananias and Sapphira, definitely not the legend.

God is not partial in His choice for replacement, what a man sows shall he reaps. The life you live now will tell whether the Lord will anoint you as a replacement for the legend or pass you by. That He might not pass you by and as many children of God as will read this book, the Lord anointed and expressly commanded me to write this book. May the Lord's purpose for writing this book be accomplished in your life in Jesus name.

Before we move to the next chapter, it is important to let you know that God is so merciful and gracious that He never stop giving man a second chance, even a third chance if there is need for it. No matter what your life is today, I tell you the truth, you are still not out of use in the plan of God. All that He is waiting for is for you to switch on the green light for God to start using you for a greater glory. As you repent of your sinful way, you cause a great joy in heaven. That simple but great action of repentance will make the angels of the Lord to give praises to the Lord, and because the Lord too will rejoice over your repentance, He will now execute His plan in your life.

"For I know the thoughts that I think toward you, saith the Lord, thoughts of peace, and not of evil, to give you an expected end" (Jeremiah 29:11)

Chapter Three

Three Powerful Experiences Needed Before Gilgal

...From Gilgal

There are places a man can go that will transform his life. A great landmark is made in his life that will make him never to remain the same throughout the rest of his life. There are also places a man can go that will mark the end of his life. Being in such places makes him an accursed; he incurs curses without knowing it. The Holy Spirit throws more light on this in the book of Psalm.

"Blessed is the man that walketh not in the counsel of the ungodly, nor standeth in the way of the sinners, nor sitteth in the seat of the scornful" (Psalm 1:1)

There is a way a man can walk that will make him blessed, there is also a way a man can stand that will count him to be part of the people blessed by the Lord. So also, a man can sit somewhere, such that he is rightly positioned for God's blessing. If the man that walks not in the counsel of the ungodly is blessed, then, the man that walks in the counsel of the ungodly is cursed by the Lord. Every word in the Bible has a purpose. The Holy Spirit would not have written such word through the men of old if they do not have particular purposes.

"And it came to pass, when the Lord would take up Elijah into heaven by a whirlwind, that Elijah went with Elisha from Gilgal" (2 Kings 2:1)

When God was ready to take Elijah away, both Elijah and Elisha left from Gilgal, that is to say, they were on their way from Gilgal. Why the mention of the name of the City called Gilgal? Any significance of this city called Gilgal in the journey of Elijah to glory as he departed from this world and in the journey of Elisha as he comes out of the crowd, being separated and ushered into glory as he receives matchless abundant anointing? However, it must be noted here that the location is not as important at all as the event that took place at the location. Therefore we must not exalt the location than the event, for it is the event that makes the location and not vice versa.

Before we can understand the significance of Gilgal in the journey of Elisha, we need to know the implications of the places they went after they left Gilgal. Through the following experiences, that we shall study—The Bethel, Jericho and Jordan experiences—God prepares and equips His people to become legends in His kingdom. There is hardly a legend in the kingdom that had not passed through these experiences.

The Bethel Experience

"And Elijah said to Elisha, Tarry here, I pray thee: for the Lord has sent me to Bethel. And Elisha said unto him, As the Lord liveth, and thy soul liveth, I will not leave thee. So they went down to Bethel". 2 Kings 2:2

On assignment, Elijah prepared to go to Bethel, so he told Elisha to stay at Gilgal. But Gilgal is not a place to stay for ever. Elijah would not want to force or even encourage Elisha to choose to go with him to Bethel. Elisha himself must decide. Bethel rang bell in the heart of Elisha. Bethel! It was the place where Abraham made his first altar to the Lord. The Lord specifically instructed Jacob to go to Bethel to build an altar to the Almighty God (Genesis 35:1)

At Bethel, Jacob saw a wonderful vision no one else had ever seen before his days and after him in the Old Testament period. Jacob was on a journey of which he was not sure of what would come out of it. He was running away from his brother Esau who had planned to kill him after the death of Isaac their father. Esau wanted to kill Jacob because Jacob had deceitfully robbed him of his blessing as firstborn child of the family. Jacob got to Bethel distressed and wretched. He was homely all his life, but now, he had to go and live with his uncle whom he had never seen. He was mummy's pet, now he would be away from his loving parents for some years. In fact, by the time he had opportunity to return back home his mother was already dead. That tells us that Jacob was embarking on a journey he lacked the knowledge of its outcome. On the journey, perhaps the first night, Jacob was at Bethel and it was dark, so he picked a stone, laid his head on it, and slept off.

"And he dreamed, and behold a ladder set up on the earth, and the top of it reached to heaven: and behold the angels of God ascending and descending on it.

And behold, the Lord stood above it, and said I am the God of Abraham thy father, and the God of Isaac:

And Jacob awaked out of his sleep, and he said, Surely the Lord is in this place: and I knew it not.

And he was afraid, and said, 'How dreadful is this place!' This is none other but the house of God, and this is the gate of heaven.

And he called the name of the place Beth-el, but the name of that city was called Luz at the first". Genesis 28: 12-19.

As Jacob slept, he saw a ladder that connected heaven with the earth. On that ladder, he saw the angels, the host of heaven ascending from the earth to heaven and descending from heaven to the earth. There was a great, speedy traffic between the heaven and the earth only via the ladder. What could that ladder be? What can we liken it to? A ladder is an aid to ascend and descend with ease. It is an aid to reach the top.

"And He saith unto him, Verily, verily, I say unto you, Hereafter ye shall see heaven open, and the angels of God ascending and descending upon the son of man". John 1:51.

Many centuries after Jacob saw the vision of open heaven, Jesus gave the interpretation in the above scriptural verse. The Son of man—Jesus—is the ladder that connects heaven with the earth. He is the Way, the only way that leads to heaven, even to the Father. Jesus is the only authentic link with the Father. He that wants to make heaven must be a friend of Jesus. No one can hate or reject the Son and still claim to know the Father. Once you see Jesus, you have invariably seen the Father. The Son is the radiance of God's glory and the exact representation of His being (Hebrews 1:3 NIV) He that will be connected with the Most High God must first be compatible with Jesus.

"Jesus saith unto him, I am the way, the truth, and the life: no man cometh unto the Father, but by me" (John 14:6)

There is no religiosity that can replace or substitute Christ Jesus in the salvation plan of God for man. In the Old Testament days, at Bethel, the Lord Jesus revealed Himself to Jacob as the ladder through whom the angels of God ascend and descend. If you need the favour of God, if the angels of God must act on your behalf, you must be connected with Jesus. From time to time in the Old Testament days, the Lord kept disclosing His identity to men and showing them how much they needed Him. His word in Proverbs 8:34-36 explains it all.

"Blessed is the man that heareth me, watching daily at my gates, waiting at the posts of my doors. For whoso findeth me findeth life, and shall obtain favour of the Lord. But he that sinneth against me wrongeth his own soul: and they that hate me love death".

Nobody that hates Jesus will make heaven. Hell remains the abode of people that reject Jesus. That great vision was revealed to Jacob at Bethel.

"And Elijah said unto Elisha, Tarry here, I pray thee; for the Lord

hath sent me to Bethel"

Elisha must have remembered Bethel to be the place where God met both Abraham the friend of God and Jacob the prince of the King of kings. Elisha would therefore not tarry at Gilgal, for he knew that with Elijah in Bethel, something great would happen; therefore he refused to be left behind. Elisha seemed to love to be in a place where the great man of God is, for in such places, the power of God is present. To show that all that Elijah wanted was for Elisha to personally decide his destiny, when Elisha insisted on following him, Elijah did not object to it.

Where do you love to be; where the crowd is or where the Lord is present? Who do you love to go out with—the lovers of God or the lovers of the world? How do you spend your leisure—on worldly things, watching unprofitable fables on Television that have nothing good to add to your life? Decisions such as these determine and shape our destiny. When the assignment at Bethel had been carried out, Elijah seemed to have asked Elisha; "Do you still want to go with me? Is your love to be the head still burning? Or are you tired and wearied because the transfer of power is taking too much time and not as fast as you might earlier have thought?"

You need revelation of the Lord

"And Elijah said unto him, Elisha, Tarry here, I pray thee; for the Lord hath sent me to Jericho"

Elijah got another assignment in Jericho but he would not force Elisha to go with him. You see, destiny is a matter of choice. Destiny is like a blank cheque, what you fill in is what you get. Jesus once said;

"Ask, and it shall be given..." Matthew 7:7

What you ask determines what you get. How much you ask is a relative of what you receive. If you ask enough you will receive enough. People that are lazy in prayer are doing a great harm against their destiny; they starve themselves of God's provision for their lives. Through laziness and ignorance, with their own hands, they put a limit to their spiritual achievement and success in life. Elisha was a man of purpose. Time would not determine whether or not he would be more or less interested in his goal. For some of us, when the desire to claim a promise is burning in our heart, we are zealous in our prayer over such needs. But as time goes on, and the requests seem not to be manifesting on the physical, then we are discouraged. Though we keep asking for it, such prayers are form of routine than prayers of faith with high expectation. But for Elisha, nothing would discourage him or reduce his eagerness to achieve what he wanted. Elijah was like asking Elisha; "Would you stay here or go with me?"

"And he said, As the Lord liveth, and thy soul liveth, I will not leave thee. So they came to Jericho". 2 Kings 2:4

Elisha had followed Elijah to Bethel, the place of revelation, where true revelation of the Lord is released to man. It is a place where man is rightly connected with the Most High. A place where all you need to get to the top, what you need do to succeed is revealed to you. A place where you see the face of your Helper, though you are faced with difficult situation, but in Bethel, you see your Helper at work and that gives you comfort and extra strength to move ahead. Let me share this testimony with you. There was a time when my wife and my children were still far away from me. I needed an apartment of my own. As I kept checking the news papers for adverts on room vacancies, I saw one apartment that was 120 Euros. I was shocked. I was shocked because I had been made to understand that the least apartment one could have would not be less than 200 Euros. I also went round to see for myself, I didn't find any that was less than 220 Euros. By the time I called for the apartment, someone had already taken it. However, I got a revelation from the Lord. *"If it was possible for an unbeliever to get that too cheap apartment, why should it be impossible for the child of God to get the same even cheaper one?"* I believed God knew where the cheapest apartments were in Vienna and God was able to lead me to such a place. If God could bring Eve from no where to Adam, I believe He could take me to that apartment. I got the revelation from God's word that says "With God all things are possible" to me, getting a cheap apartment is part of all things that are possible with God.

Everyone I informed about my search for apartment asked me the price range I wanted, and then I would tell them, "The one that is not more than 120 EURO per month". Many of them told me; "Brother Gbenga, that is not possible, unless you will get an apartment in a dilapidated building" However, many that had no boldness only nodded their heads but they never made any attempt to search for "impossible apartment" for me. But each time it occurred to me that I needed a cheap apartment, I would tell God, "Lord, with men this is impossible, however, your word says but not with God for with God all things are possible". Friends, indeed, it was possible with God. The apartment I got was 117:61 Euros. While many people saw with human eyes which could only see limitation and impossibility, I had the grace to see with the eyes of the spirit. That is what Bethel is, rather than letting you to see what the enemy is doing, it enables you to see what God is doing on your behalf. Why do you think it is easy for many people to doubt and lose hope? Simply because they do not see their Helper (God) working on their behalf. All they could see is what the devil or their enemies are doing.

Elisha needed revelation to succeed in his ministry. He needed to see with the eye of the spirit, not as man sees, rather as God would see. Any man of God that lacks revelation is like a man that proposed to marry a dark skinned lady sitting in the dark. The man could not see her face, yet he married her even in the dark. In the light, anyone can claim to be that woman once the person can pretend to be like that woman in the dark. A child of God that lacks the revelation of the Lord can easily be deceived by the angels of darkness that disguise like angels of light. You need the revelation of the Master, the Lord Jesus Christ.

"I keep asking that the God of our Lord Jesus Christ, the glorious Father, may give you the spirit of wisdom and revelation, so that you may know Him better" Ephesians 1:17

Revelation of the Lord will help you to know the Lord *better*. You know Him already, but you can still know Him better. Not just knowing Him *more*, rather *better*. Revelation of the Lord helps you to be sure of who you believe. It will help you to trust in Him to the point of committing your spirit in His hand even when it seems He has forsaken you. When pains, tribulations, among others strive to force you to deny your faith, the personal revelation of the Lord that you have will help you to say like Paul;

"Who shall separate us from the love of Christ? Shall tribulation or distress, or persecution or famine, or nakedness or peril, or sword?

He proceeded by saying;

For I am persuaded, that neither death, nor life, nor angels, nor principalities, nor powers, nor things present, nor things to come,

Nor height, nor depth, nor any other creature, shall be able to separate us from the love of God, which is in Christ Jesus our Lord" (Romans 8:38, 39)

The revelation of the Lord will help you in no small way to really be in love with the Lord. That love of God will make you not to fear tribulation, distress, persecution, poverty, sickness and death, rather, you fear only the Lord. Revelation of the Lord helps you to see solution when other people see problem situations. In the Second Kings Chapter six, the Syrian army surrounded the city where Elisha and his servants were.

"And when the servant of the man of God was risen early, and gone forth, behold, an host compassed the city both with horses and chariots. And his servant said unto him, Alas, my master! How shall we do?" (82 Kings 6:15)

The servant saw the enemies, multitude of enemies surrounding them, but what did Elisha see? Elisha did not see the mountain surrounded by the enemies. Rather, he saw the mountain filled by the horses and chariots *of fire* sent by God. Christians that lack the revelation of the Lord are prone to seeing demons threatening them. They always see the devil working against them. When a Christian lacks the revelation of the Lord, the devil sends in to him his own revelation. While the revelation of the Lord stirs up faith in you that of the devil brings fear. and we know that fear has torment.

At another time in 2 Kings 4:38-41, the sons of the prophets were having lunch with Elisha, suddenly they discovered that the cook mistakenly included poisonous herbs in the food, though they were prophets-in training, they cried out;

"There is death in the pot"

They saw death in the pot, but Elisha saw a different thing, he saw life, he saw solution to the problem at hand. We need the revelation of the Lord that we may indeed walk by faith and not by sight.

"Cease not to give thanks for you, making mention of you in my prayer; that the God of our Lord Jesus Christ, the Father of glory, may give you the spirit of wisdom and revelation in the knowledge of Him" (Ephesians 1: 16, 17)

The Jericho Experience

The revelation of the Lord will prepare you for an enduring victory. If you still fear the followings; life challenges, what the enemy is planning against you everyday without ceasing and the threat of the kingdom of darkness, friend, you surely need Jericho experience if you will indeed become a legend. After Bethel assignment, both Elijah and Elisha got to Jericho. Of course, Jericho was a quite different place. Jericho was a place of victory without human effort. It is a venue of victory, where the heavenly host fights for the sakes of the children of God.

When the Israelites left the wilderness, they got to the border of a fortified city. The Lord had given the land to the Israelites but the people of Jericho would not lose their land just like that. They therefore built a thick wall round the city.

"Now Jericho was straitly shut up because of the children of Israel: none went out and none came in. And the Lord said unto Joshua, See, I have given into thine hand Jericho, and the king thereof, and the mighty men of valour." Joshua 6:1-2

The Lord gave the Israelites this instruction: all the men of war would go round the city once a day for six days. On the seventh day however, they would walk round the city seven times. At the seventh time, the priests shall blow the trumpets, the people shall shout with a great shout and the wall shall fall down flat. Simple won't you say! That the wall would fall down flat as a result of walking round about it, and making a great shout should not make you to think that the wall was tiny or weak.

After Rahab had been kind to the Israeli spies, she requested that her parents and relatives be saved, then, the Bible has this description about her house.

"Then she let them down by a cord through the window: for her house was upon the town wall, and she dwelt upon the wall." Joshua 2:15

The wall of Jericho was so wide that a brothel could be built upon it. It was probably the thickest, widest wall ever built round a city, just wide enough to have a building erected upon it. As big and wide the wall of Jericho was, to destroy it, the Israelites would just walk round about it and make a great shout. The Lord was invariably saying that the battle was His. While God's people were matching round the wall without anything in their hands, the people dwelling in Jericho saw them; they felt they were secured because of the wall that could have taken them months or years to build. It was not impossible for them to have mocked the Israelites. But really, here the Lord told us that the battle in the lives of God's people, are not fought by men of flesh and blood, but by the angels of God. Think of this—what can be the size of the wall that the enemies have built to hinder you from reaching your goal? What are the things your adversaries are doing from time to time to frustrate your efforts thereby standing before you and your joy? While God's people were matching round the wall of Jericho, I suppose the angels were busy destroying the foundations of the wall.

Prior to the first day of walking round about the wall, the captain of the Lord's army had visited Joshua.

"Now when Joshua was near Jericho, he looked up and saw a man standing in front of him with a drawn sword in his hand. Joshua went up to him and asked, 'Are you for us or our enemies? Neither, he replied, but as commander of the army of the Lord I have now come. Then Joshua fell face down to the ground in reverence, and asked him, What message does my Lord have for his servant?" (Joshua 5:13-14) NIV

The commander of the army of the Lord came to Joshua ahead of the time of the war. The coming of the commander of the army of the

Lord tells us that the army of the Lord was already present there. Now, the children of God walked round the wall seven times on the seventh day, as they made great shout, the army of the Lord, led by their commander pulled down the wall flat. Jericho was the place where the heavens fight on behalf of man.

Elisha surely understood what Jericho stood for in his journey, he knew that revelation from the Lord without the Lord fighting the battle for man, man is incomplete and useless, and therefore, Elisha showed his willingness to follow Elijah to Jericho. Hence, they both went to Jericho while Elijah performed the assignment sent him.

"And Elijah said unto him, Tarry, I pray thee, here; for the Lord hath sent me to Jordan" (2 Kings 2:6)

The Jordan Experience

Elijah told Elisha to stay in Jericho while he went to Jordan for another assignment. Tarry, I pray thee, here in Jericho, in the land of victory, Elijah told Elisha. But, Elisha would not, for where the anointed man of God is, there Elisha wanted to be. The man of God is the temple of the Holy Spirit. There is no temple without an altar, and our heart is the altar on which we make daily sacrifices and offerings in the form of thanksgiving to the Lord. A place is not called a temple if there is no spirit living there. Therefore, the Holy Spirit dwells in our body. The child of God is not just the carrier of the Holy Spirit, he also carries everything you can find in the Holy Spirit. He carries the anointing, the gifts and the power of the Holy Spirit. Wherever such a person is, the heaven pays attention to such a place. Elisha knew that Elijah was never alone; he therefore would not want anything to separate them until his heart desire is fully granted.

In our Christian journey, the Lord teaches us many things, but one after the other. For Elisha, apart from Gilgal, he went to Bethel, then to Jericho and finally to Jordan. Many are Christians, when they behold the glory of God, the blessings attached to holiness, perfection and righteousness in Gilgal, they are so glad and appreciate the Lord. But as the Lord tells them about going to Bethel, they begin to make comparison and say; "Lord, we are satisfied with

Gilgal. Holiness is enough for us". They reject invitation to Bethel— the place of revelation. Ask them what they know about their faith, nothing but holiness you will discover.

For other Christians, they walk with the Lord to Bethel, due to the glory of the revelations; they would not want to move forward. For some other Christians, they followed the Lord to all these places, surprisingly, they just choose one, and then they claim to be Preachers of holiness. Another person claims "I am a preacher of faith" While someone else says; "I am a deliverance minister"

But the Lord does not take us to these places that we may have choices, rather that we may possess them all! Thank God for the life of Elisha, he possessed all. That is the man that is ready to fulfil all the will of God for his life.

What is the significance of Jordan in the journey of Elisha? Why go with Elijah to Jordan?

"And the Lord said unto Joshua, This day will I begin to magnify thee in the sight of all Israel, that they may know that, as I was with Moses, so I will be with thee.

And thou shall command the priests that bear the ark of the covenant, saying, When ye are come to the brink of the water of Jordan, ye shall stand still in Jordan.

And Joshua said unto the children of Israel, Come hither, and hear the words of the Lord your God.

And Joshua said, Hereby ye shall know that the living God is among you, and that He will without fail drive out from before you the Canaanites, and Hittites, and the Hivites, and the Perizzites, and the Girgashites, and the Amorites, and the Jebusites.

Behold, the ark of the covenant of the Lord of all the earth passeth over before you into Jordan. Now therefore take you twelve men out of the tribes of Israel, out of every tribe a man.

And it shall come to pass, as soon as the soles of the feet of the priests that bear the ark of the Lord, the Lord of all the earth, shall rest in the waters of Jordan, that the waters of Jordan shall be cut off from the waters that come down from above; and they shall stand upon an heap.

And it came to pass, when the people removed from their tents, to pass over Jordan, and the priests bearing the ark of the covenant before the people;

And as they that bear the ark were come unto Jordan, and the feet of the priests that bare the ark were dipped in the brim of the water, (for Jordan overfloweth all his banks all the time of harvest,)

That the waters which came down from above stood and rose up upon an heap very far from the city Adam, that is beside Zaretan: and those that came down toward the sea of the plain, even the salt sea, failed, and were cut off: and the people passed over right against Jericho.

And the priests that bear the ark of the covenant of the Lord stood firm on dry ground in the midst of Jordan, and all the Israelites passed over on dry ground, until all the people were passed clean over Jordan." Joshua 3:7-17

Jordan was a river that got its waters from many sources, hence the Bible referred to it as the waters of Jordan. The Israelites were on their way from the wilderness to the promised-land. In the days of Moses, they had once walked through the sea when Moses lifted up the rod of the Lord. But the waters of Jordan would not be crossed through the same method of raising the rod. According to the instructions given to Joshua, the priests that carried the ark of the Lord would lead the procession. As soon as the feet of the priests touched the edge of the waters of Jordan, then the waters from the upstream stopped flowing; it pilled up in a heap at a great distant away, while the water flowing down the sea of the Salt Sea was completely cut off. The priests who carried the ark of the covenant of the Lord stood firm on the dry ground in the middle of the Jordan, while all the Israelites passed by until the whole nation had completed the crossing on dry ground.

Jordan was a place of faith, where a step of faith taken brings unbelievable breakthrough, progress and success. The waters of Jordan only stopped flowing when the priests had dipped their feet into the edge of the waters. Jordan teaches us about faith, that faith demonstrated on the word of God never brings failure or shame but glory. The waters could not drag away the priests, for they carried the ark of the presence of the Lord. A Christian filled with the Holy Spirit also carries the presence of the Lord. When difficulties and challenges come, a step of faith taken by such a Christian will lead to the manifestation of the glory of the Lord. That was Jordan, just take the step of faith, and success will follow. Do not walk by sight, by what you see and hear people say, rather, walk by faith, by what the Lord says.

At Jordan, only a step of faith taken gives you a great wonderful breakthrough. Elisha was never disturbed by anything called problem. He was never moved by problems, rather, he moved the problems away through the demonstration of his faith in the Lord. He was a man of faith indeed. There was a time he loved to repay the Shunammite woman for her generosity towards him. Elisha called the woman and said to her;

"Behold thou hast been careful for us with all this care; what is to be done for thee? Wouldest thou be spoken for to the king, or to the captain of the host? And she answered, I dwell among my people." 2 Kings 4:13.

The woman was wealthy, so she did not need money or compensation from the king. She was a generous woman among her people therefore she needed no protection from the captain of the army of Israel. Invariably, the woman was saying to Elisha; "Man of God, you have nothing to give me. I've already have all that man can give to another as gift". Then Elisha turned to Gehazi his servant.

"And he said, What else to be done for her..."

Elisha believed that with the anointing of the Lord upon him, there must be something he could give to the woman. Supposing God was to come to the woman, could it be that the woman is so blessed that God would have nothing special to give to her which she would appreciate and celebrate for the rest of her life? If he carries the anointing, which is God's deposit in man that enables man to act and perform through the power of God, therefore, there must be a way to bless the woman in return.

"...And Gehazi answered, Verily she hath no child, and her

husband is old"

Immediately Elisha heard the word of Gehazi, he told his servant Gehazi to call the woman in for a word. Well, the woman came but stood at the doorway. Then Elisha looked eye to eye with the woman and confidently prophesied into her life saying

"About this season, according to the time of life, thou shall embrace a son"

The woman could not believe Elisha. Perhaps she thought; "Could it be that easy?" Perhaps, Elisha was not the first man of God she had met. The truth is, the woman did not believe Elisha, for she said, "No, my lord" she objected. "Don't mislead your servant, O man of God!" Invariably, she was calling the man of God a liar! But I tell you, her faithlessness was not capable of nullifying the word of faith spoken by Elisha. For Elisha, the faith of the woman was irrelevant. Think of this: when Elisha cursed the youth that threatened his life by insulting him immediately he received the double portion anointing, supposed some of the children did not believe his word, would their faith or faithlessness have any effect on the curse he pronounced on them? Of course not. How much more when Elisha blessed with all his heart someone that had been a blessing to him!

Can you imagine, he was even specific on the sex of the child? Mind you, Elisha did not pray, there was no vision showed him concerning that either, but because that was what he wanted, he spoke the word of faith, and not even the faithlessness of the woman could nullify the word of this man called Elisha. In many more instances, the Bible tells us of many miracles performed by Elisha that tell us that he was a man of faith.

You need the revelation of the Lord to serve as your sure foundation and to prepare you for Jordan experience. You need the support of the Lord to win the battles of life, to be a winner all the time. You equally need faith to maintain and continue to abide and enjoy more the goodness of the Lord. That is what makes you famous in the kingdom. These experiences exclude you from being among the people that struggle to succeed either in secular assignment or in the ministry.

All these three locations were with a purpose in the life of Elisha. Bethel is the place of remarkable, excellent, glorious, highest revelation. For there is no revelation, that is greater than the revelation of Christ Jesus. Though Elisha was a full time farmer turned Prophet, in his ministry, revelation distinguished him from other prophets in the Bible. No problem brought to him lacked solution. Almost nothing was hidden to him, through wonderful revelation he excelled in his ministry.

Jericho is the place of victory, where the heavenly hosts fight for the sakes of men of God. Throughout the time of his ministry, Elisha never suffered oppression, insult, attack or arrest. Prophet Elisha had a long career that spanned the reigns of six kings in Israel, the Lord satisfied him with long life. When the enemies came to attack him, chariots of fire and horses of fire would round him about. It was the Lord that kept fighting his battles.

Chapter Four
The Gilgal Experience

Before Elijah and Elisha could go to Bethel, Jericho and Jordan, they had been to Gilgal. In another word, they did not go to Bethel, Jericho and Jordan until they had first gone to Gilgal. Thus, going to Gilgal preceded their journey to Bethel, Jericho and Jordan. Anybody that will move up from the crowd to the class of the legends will have to experience Gilgal.

The Place of Circumcision.

Gilgal was a place near Jericho, it was where Joshua set up twelve stones as a remembrance of the power of God (Joshua 4:19). Gilgal was the place where the children of Israel were circumcised by Joshua.

Now this is the reason Joshua circumcised them. All those who came out of Egypt—all the men of military age—died in the desert. All the people that came out had been circumcised, but all the people born in the desert during their forty-year journey from Egypt had not. These were the ones Joshua circumcised (Joshua 5:4-7).

Gilgal is a place where the child of God must be circumcised in the heart, in other for him to suit the calling which God had given him. By the reason of the circumcision of the heart, the reproach of the enemies is rolled away.

"And the Lord said unto Joshua, This day have I rolled away the reproach of Egypt from off you. Wherefore the name of the place is called Gilgal unto this day" (Joshua 5:9)

As the Israelites left Egypt, the reproach of the enemies was still on them. Even when they had passed through the Red Sea on dry ground, they still were carrying the reproach of the enemies. Though they fought many wars and overcame, the reproach of the enemies was still upon them. They had wonderful provisions in the wilderness, the miracles of manna and water from the rock; still they were not without the reproach of the enemies. But when they were circumcised, the Lord rolled away the reproach. This simply teaches us that, the fact that we receive miracles from the Lord does not mean we have no reproach of the enemies in our lives. But that reproach will be rolled away as we lay our hearts on the altar of the Lord for circumcision. Ask yourself this question; "Have I really been to Gilgal?" There are many Christians crying to the Lord for the anointing, they greatly desire and pray fervently for the Spirit of revelation, they want the hand of the Lord to wrought victory on their behalf, they desire that the Lord will bless them with great faith. They listen to sermon messages on audio and video tapes of many great preachers of the Word. They read many Christian literatures written on such subjects. They tried what the preachers prescribed, yet there seems to be no result.

God will not release His abundant, overflowing anointing on the servants of the devil, no, He will not give such to people that will not obey Him. You must be circumcised in the heart. Yes, your heart must be circumcised!

"And the Lord thy God will circumcise thine heart, and the heart of thy seed, to love the Lord thy God with all thine heart, and with all thine soul, that thou mayest live" (Deuteronomy 30:6).

Moses prophesied into the time the Lord would Himself

49

circumcise the hearts of the children of Israel, the children of God. The Lord God will take it upon Himself to circumcise men for a purpose; that they may love the Lord God **with all** their heart and **with all** their soul.

"*Jesus answered and said unto him, If a man love me, he will keep my words He that loveth me not keepeth not my sayings*" (John 14:23,24).

By this, the Lord is saying that, whoever claims to love Him must obey His word. That is, your total obedience to the word of God is a sure proof, evidence that you love Him. However, it is difficult for any man to obey the word of the Lord, His commandment, unless his heart is circumcised.

The Lord commanded Joshua to circumcise all the people before they could enter the promised-land. This teaches us that no one whose heart is not circumcised will enter the kingdom of God.

"*Jesus said unto him, Thou shall love the Lord thy God with all thy heart and with all thy soul, and with all thy mind.*

This is the first and the great commandment.

The second is like unto it, Thou shall love thy neighbour as thyself. On these two commandments hang all the law and the prophets" (Matthew 22:37-40).

The law, which is the word of God, the prophets which also refers to all the prophetic words of the men of old recorded in the Bible *hang* on these two commandments. Before the word of God and the word of prophecies by the men of old can work successfully for us, we must be lovers of God and our neighbours. The word of God and the prophets hang on these two commandments of God. For the promises of God to be fulfilled in the life of a man, he must first fulfil the commandments. If you love God you will not derive pleasure in doing what will not make Him happy. You will obey Him and not harm your neighbour either. However, God knows pretty well that unless the heart of man is circumcised he can not love the Lord God. Hence, the Lord Himself will circumcise His people, they that will surrender their hearts for circumcision.

Circumcision – A Painful Experience

It must be mentioned here that, circumcision is a painful process. Take for instance when the first skin of the flesh is cut off, it is so painful that the man loses all his strength. In Genesis 34, a young man by name Shechem the Hivite raped Dinah the only daughter of Jacob. He deliberately did this shameful act so that he could have opportunity to marry Dinah. Jacob did not say much, he had become a changed person then, for it occurred after he had met the Lord and had his name changed. But the brothers of Dinah were unhappy. They therefore told Hamor the father of Shechem, who was also the ruler of that city, that, Dinah could only marry Shechem if all the males in that city would be circumcised. On hearing this, Hamor went out to convince the people of his city, and all the males, babies, young and old were circumcised.

"And it came to pass on the third day, when they were sore, that two of the sons of Jacob, Simeon and Levi, Dinah's brethren, took each man his sword, and came upon the city boldly, and slew all the males" (Genesis 34:25).

Only two men slew all the males in a city, just two men defeated a whole city. Two men were able to kill all male babies, all the boys, all the young men and the old men in the city! It became possible because of the pain from the circumcision. Circumcision involves pains. When the Lord begins to circumcise your heart, pains are attached.

The circumcision of the heart is performed by the word of God. Immediately we become born-again, the Lord is set to start the circumcision of our hearts. The only thing He needs from us is co-operation, total surrender of our hearts on the altar, for He will not struggle or use force as He carries out the circumcision.

The Milk-Word

As we give our lives to Jesus, we are babes in the Lord, and the Lord starts the circumcision work by feeding us with the milk of His word. Milk as it is, is the easiest food a baby can take, that also digest so quickly and easily. Hence, milk is the first food of a baby.

"As newly born babes, desire the sincere milk of the word, that ye may grow thereby" (1 Peter 2:2).

As milk is liquid, soft, and easy to take and also digests easily, so is the word with which the Lord feeds a newly born Christian. He feeds him with the word that is easily understood and easy for the man to accept.

"…That ye *may grow* thereby".

The milk word is meant for growth. Therefore, there is the need to move up away from the realm of a baby-Christian. It is sad to hear and see some people claiming to have given their lives to Jesus, attending churches for decades, yet they remain baby Christians. It is important to say here that, there is danger remaining too long in this milk-word realm. For the salvation chance of a baby Christian is 50-50.The chance he has to make heaven is the same chance he has to lose heaven.

Let us search the scriptures to know who a baby Christian really is.

"And I, brethren, could not speak unto you as unto spiritual, but as unto carnal, even as unto babes in Christ, I have fed you with milk and not with meat, for hitherto ye were not able to bear it, neither yet now are ye able.

Ye are yet Carnal: for whereas there is among you envying, and strive, and divisions, are ye not carnal, and walk as men?" (I Corinthians 3:1-3).

As Paul ministered to the church in Corinth, he could not go deep into the word of God, for the people were babes in Christ. An attempt to go deep into interpretation of the scripture, the people would be confused and lost. Digging deep into the scripture before such people is like feeding an eight-day old baby with solid food. That is the first reason why it is not good to remain in that milk-word realm for too long. For there you have little understanding and you are not qualified to receive deep things of God.

"Whom shall He teach knowledge? And whom shall He make to understand doctrine? Them that are weaned from the milk, and drawn from the breasts" (Isaiah 28:9)

A babe in Christ has little or no knowledge and understanding of what he believes. If you question his faith, he will not be able to answer until he hears from his pastor or the Sunday School Bible teacher. Such people quote their pastors rather than what the Lord says. But the Lord will teach them knowledge and grant them understanding when they are weaned and drawn away from the breasts. A baby Christian has not reached a stage where he can receive knowledge and understanding of the deep things of God.

Apostle Paul was frank in his writing to the church at Corinth, saying he could only speak to them as he would speak to people that is yet carnal. A carnal person is an unbeliever, a sinner. The difference between a carnal and a babe in Christ is that the latter has confessed and accepted Jesus as his personal Lord and Saviour.

"For ye are yet Carnal: for whereas there is among you envying and strife, and divisions, are ye not carnal, and walk as men?"

A baby Christian, just as a carnal man, still harbours in his heart the spirit of envy. They are jealous of others and quick to compare themselves with others. When someone achieves greater things than them, then they begin to envy such a person. They do not see anything wrong in fighting someone that stirs up their anger. To them, there is nothing bad even fighting in the church. Worst still, they cause divisions in the church of God. They do this because they lack knowledge of who they are as Christians; they have no understanding of what they do. If they die or rapture happened while they were in such state, they will miss heaven. Such were the people in the Church at Corinth that wanted to set Paul, Apollos and Peter against one another when they began to announce, "I love and prefer Peter", the other person would say, "I prefer Paul", and someone else would say, "Apollos is my choice". They bring stumbling blocks before the men of God. Some of them fight as they return from Church even with their Bible in their hands, and the unbeliever would say: "And you say that you go to church". The name of the Lord and the gospel is blasphemed through them.

"For every one that useth milk is unskilful in the word of righteousness; for he is a babe."

What a terrible state to be for too long. A babe in Christ is unskillful in the word of righteousness. When it comes to using the word of God to produce result, babes in Christ are unskilful. They read the Bible, but they can not rightly apply the word to their situation. Until they see the pastor, their problem remains. To them, the Bible is like a history book. The promises of God to Abraham, for instance is like they are for Abraham alone, and when God rebuked the Israelites, they are not aware that the Lord was rebuking them as well if they were doing the same thing. They lack knowledge of the use of the word of God.

The Meat-Word

This is where the difference between the milk-word and meat-word begins to show. Meat is stronger than milk, and it is difficult for a baby to take. Immediately the milk gets into your mouth, you can swallow it, but that is not the same with meat. Nobody will feed you, you do it yourself. You need to cut it to the size you desire, as it gets into your mouth, you do not swallow but masticate it well with your teeth and the help of the saliva already provided for you by your Creator right in your mouth. The meat-word demands more from you.

Just immediately a new convert moves up from the milk-word realm, the Lord begins to feed him with meat-word. It is the rejection of the meat-word that makes someone to remain in the milk-word realm. The message that he receives as he listens to sermons and as he studies his Bible will change. This is the realm where he is taught to do the will of God. Jesus once told His disciples;

"...My meat is to do the will of Him that sent me, and to finish His work" (John 4:34).

Yes, in the above scriptural verse, the word meat means food. However, Jesus chose to use meat rather than bread which was commonly being used in those days. The meat-word realm is where God's children are trained to do the will of the Lord which they have learnt about in the milk-word realm. The Lord will teach him to pray at all times. He will demand this because the Lord wants to hear from him at all times. Likewise too, the Lord wants to talk to him at all times and teach him knowledge; therefore, he must study, not just read but study the word of God day and night. This is the major hurdle that makes many to return to milk-word realm, for they do not have time for Bible study and personal prayer. But for those that surrender to the Lord, as they study the word of God, they will discover that the word demands that they be not hearers alone but doers. As they accept to be the doers of the word, they discover that they must be holy, forgive their offenders, be merciful, pay the tithe of their income, preach the word, and win souls and fellowship with fellow children of God. They get to know that they need to deny themselves of sleep in other to keep vigil. As the Lord gives them the knowledge of these, He will also grant them the understanding of the reasons they must do them, that is, the blessings attached to obedience of such demands.

The pains in circumcision begin to show now. Maybe you do not joke with your sleep, spending over one third of your life to sleep. You can imagine, if we sleep for eight hours every day, and maintain that for thirty years, we would have spent over ten years sleeping all alone! But now, the Lord demands that you should cease to be a slave to sleep. You can't just sleep because sleep demands it. Rather, you should now control your sleep. That is a pain of circumcision to cope with. The Lord is not going to rush all these to you at once, but gradually, one after the other. The level of your obedience and readiness to submit to His will and accept His word will determine how long a time you will spend in the meat-word realm.

Strong Meat-Word

"But strong meat belongeth to them that are of full age, even those by reason of use have their senses exercised to discern both good and evil" (Hebrews 5:14).

If wrongly understood, the intention of the Lord as He feeds us with the meat-word could be taken to mean getting devoted, being religious, becoming active in the church programmes and activities without focus on holiness.

However, as the Lord feeds you with strong meat-word, He begins to speak and instruct you personally. He looks into your personal life and points out to you certain habits you must stop even though before now you did not consider them sinful. The word of

God begins to shift your love from the things of the world to the Lord. He will demand from you to sacrifice Isaac that you love unto Him in other to test your obedience and your steadfast love for the Lord. The word of God begins to tell you that you can not speak any how, like some people, rather as God's people. He tells you to dress like the children of His kingdom not like heathen.

This is the realm of holiness, where the word of God coming to you lays more emphasis on holiness, sanctification and perfection. This is where the Lord, through His word, purges and cleanses you of all unrighteousness and anything called sin. It is always where your total obedience to the word and the voice of God is fully required. Without any prior notice, the word of God may tell you to go on fasting for some days. But you say "Lord, I do not have it in my agenda to fast today!" He did it for Jesus. After water baptism, without preparation, the Holy Spirit led Him into the wilderness. He did not know before hand how many days He would spend, the fasting and prayer did not finish until the Holy Spirit said it was finished. You could just wake up at the middle of the night while the Spirit tells you to study the word of God. "Oh, what an odd time!" You might say. But it is the right time in the sight of the Lord, for then the Lord is near. All these are strong meat. They are strong because they demand more from you.

The word may come to you so clearly that you sell your only car to fund evangelism. What a strong meat! For everyone that hears that will say you are out of your mind. The mother and the brothers of Jesus once said this concerning Jesus; "*He is out of His mind*" (Mark 3:21 NIV). For Apostle Paul, they said; "*...Much learning doth make thee mad*" (Acts 26:24).

The strong meat-word could be that the Lord keeps telling you to turn to a full-time minister of God. But you think the time is not yet ripe for that, for you have not made adequate preparation for that. What a strong meat. So, you probably think that you are more knowledgeable than the Lord. The strong meat-word could be like that which came to Philip that he should go to the way of the wilderness. He should have told the Lord; Why the way of wilderness Lord? For the people that pass through the way were travellers. They hardly have time to listen to sermon. Even if they grant you audience, you cannot carryout any follow-up on such converts. Evangelism in the city is better than in the way of wilderness. Philip could have "taught" the Lord as most of us sometimes do. But Philip had submitted his total life to the Lord. He obeyed and his obedience earned him what anybody else before him and after him in the Bible days never had. The Holy Spirit that he obeyed became a vehicle that took him from one city to another. In this realm, you receive from the word of God what you may consider as strong teaching. But if you will only submit to the Lord totally, your success in this realm will launch you to the next realm which is glorious.

Honey-word

"Therefore the Lord himself will give you a sign; Behold, a virgin shall conceive, and bear a son, and shall call His name Immanuel.

Butter and honey shall he eat, that he may know to refuse the evil, and choose the good" (Isaiah 7:14, 15).

After we have shown complete and unceasing obedience to both the meat-word and strong meat-word, every word of the Lord that comes to us becomes as sweet as honey. At this point, we care less about our personal interests. We are only concerned about the interest of the Lord. As we allow the commandment of the Lord to become honey, the Lord too makes His word in our mouth to be as honey. Every word we pronounce is seen and treated as the word of the Lord.

After the wall of Jericho had fallen, then Joshua said these words;

"Cursed be the man before the Lord, that riseth up and build this city Jericho: he shall lay the foundation thereof in his firstborn, and in his youngest son shall he set up the gate of it" (Joshua 6:26).

However, many years later, we have this testimony;

"In his days did Hiel the Beth-elite build Jericho: he laid the foundation thereof in Abiram his firstborn, and set up the gates thereof in his youngest son Segub, according to the word of the Lord, which He spake by Joshua son of Nun" (I Kings 16:34).

Every word of faith and word of prayer spoken by the child of God that operates in honey-word realm automatically becomes the word of the Lord. Isaiah 44:24-26 tell us that the Lord confirms the word of His servant and performs the counsel of His messengers. Therefore, as you live your life in conformity with His word, the Lord too has a task to confirm your word and perform your counsel. Let us read the above scripture in the New International Version for clearer meaning.

"Who carries out the word of His servants and fulfils the predictions of His messengers,..."

This is exactly what the Lord is doing concerning His legends. Even when they pray for twenty seconds, great miracles would follow. Thus, we are amazed. They may preach for just ten minutes quoting just one verse from the Bible, yet, when they make altar call, so many people would give their lives to Jesus. The simple word spoken by them touch the hearts of the people greatly including people you think it would be difficult to convert, such people burst into tears as they accept Jesus into their lives. And in our heart we begin to wonder what was special in the sermon that was delivered. But really, the word that came out was no more the word of man, but the word that carried the power of God. Having replaced their will with the Lord's, God becomes the performer of their word. He acts fast to fulfil their prophetic utterances. If we allow the word of God which is sharper than any two-edged sword to circumcise our heart, honey-realm awaits us. Honey realm is the dwelling realm of the legends, and it is accessed through total submission to the word of God. Thus, God circumcises our hearts through His word. Circumcision is important if we must become one of the legends of the Lord.

Celebration of God's Goodness

"And the children of Israel encamped in Gilgal, and kept the Passover on the fourteenth day of the month at even in the plains of Jericho" (Joshua 5:10).

After the circumcision of every male Israelite, then the people celebrated the Passover, they remembered the goodness and the favour of the Lord. When they were in Egypt, while the destroying angel smote all the firstborn of the Egyptians, he passed over Goshen where the children of Israel lived. Thus, Gilgal is a land or that period of time in your spiritual life where and when you learn to remember the goodness of the Lord. Where you learn to count your blessings and not your loses. The Israelites did not remember their sufferings in Egypt, and the loss of all their parents in the wilderness, rather they celebrated the faithfulness of the Lord which they enjoyed in the land of Egypt. At this stage of your walk with the Lord, you will need to learn how to count your blessings and not your losses. This is where you begin to thank God for what He had done for you and not feel sad for what He has not done. You see, many Christians have missed their blessing because of their ignorance on this issue. It does not matter how terrible your life may be right now. The truth is, what you do now will determine whether your situation will improve or deteriorate. Let us learn a lesson from the birth of Jesus.

Luke 2 has this record about the birth of Jesus. During a census period, Joseph and Mary travelled to Jerusalem in order to be counted. However, when they got to the hotel, the lodging officer told them there was no more room, and so, he turned them back. Yet, Mary was heavy. She was about to deliver the baby of whom the angel said would be called Jesus, the Son of the Living God. The only place open to Mary and Joseph to stay was a place where sheep were being reared. In that dirty environment, Jesus was born. No bed available to place the child, other than the manger. Now, many who are not familiar with animal rearing may not know what manger is. Manger is simply a container through or from which animals eat their food. Think of this, the greatest man that ever lived was born and placed in the manger. Should the angels of God be happy at the delivery of this so called "good-news"?

But indeed, when an angel came to the shepherd to inform them of the birth of Christ, suddenly, great number of angels descended, they formed the first mass choir and sang the first Christmas song. (Luke 2:13-14). Notwithstanding where Jesus was born, the angels were happy. The truth is, you must not allow your joy to be determined by what is happening in your life, by what you have, by what you do not have or by your feelings. That God is for us should always stir joy from within us. As it later turned out, the fact that Jesus was born in a manger did not mean He would die in a manger. That He was born by poor, non influential parents did not mean Jesus would not make it in life. Many are sad because they were not born by rich parents, therefore no matter what God is doing in their lives, once they remember the disadvantage of being born by poor parents, they lose their joy. Another truth is that, you couldn't have been born in a better nation than where you were born, because, the fact that you were born poor does not mean you will die poor. Jesus did not for once make a reference to the manger where He was born. He fixed His gaze to where He would end His journey, His goal in life. People who fix their gaze on what they lack never really have reason to serve the Lord with joy and gladness. You can see them around in the Church. It does not matter what their roles are, they may be members of the choir, yet, they would sing joyful songs with sorrow written all over their faces. This action is capable of stopping the flow of God's blessing into their lives. Not only that, it also opens up curses.

"Because thou servedst not the Lord thy God with joyfulness, and with gladness of heart, for the abundance of all things;

Therefore shalt thou serve thine enemies which the Lord shall send against thee, in hunger, and in thirst, and in nakedness, and in want of all things: and he shall put a yoke of iron upon thy neck, until he have destroyed thee" (Deuteronomy 28:47-48).

Where joy and gladness cease to flow, curses spring up. No matter what you may be passing through right now, which may be considered enough for you to feel sad, if you will think deep, there are certain things in your life which signify the goodness of the Lord. If you can not find anything, how about the step God took, whereby He gave His only Son to die on the cross that you might be saved from spending eternity in hell? At least you have a future, a future to spend eternity with God. Many people born at the time of your birth have died under different circumstances, that you are alive means you still have opportunity to enjoy the goodness of God. At Gilgal, you must begin to celebrate the goodness of God in your life, and not magnify the enemy by considering what you have lost. Consider this, if your life is like this even when you have God as your defence, what do you think the devil would have turned your life into if God were not to be for you? However, God is ready to show you more of His faithfulness if you will walk in His way which is serving Him with joy and gladness. Why must you move from blessing to curses and then back to blessing only to return to curses, when in actual fact, you can live permanently in the midst of blessing? In the time of your prosperity do not forget to serve God with joy and gladness. Even when you think prosperity is far from you, you can still move the hand of God to work for your sake through serving and praising Him with gladness and joy. That was exactly what Paul and Silas did.

At the birth of Jesus, the angels knew that the end of a matter is more important than the beginning, therefore, they rejoiced even when the King of kings was born and placed in manger. Can you imagine, it was like categorising Him along with the animals! But for the angels, that situation was nothing compared to the glory to come. At Gilgal, the Israelites of old were taught to celebrate God's goodness. They learnt to count their blessings, to appreciate God for what He had done and not what He left undone. Anybody that will walk his ways to the class of the legends of the Lord must cultivate the habit of celebrating God's goodness.

At Gilgal Manna Stopped

"And the manna ceased on the morrow after they had eaten of the old corn of the land; neither had the children of Israel manna any more; but they did eat of the fruit of the land of Canaan that year" (Joshua 5:12).

Just when they celebrated the Passover, the manna stopped to fall from heaven. Before now, for forty years they had been eating free food called manna. All they needed do was to go out everyday close to their camp, gather food meant for that day. For forty years, they neither sown nor reaped, yet they had a table prepared for them in the wilderness.

At Gilgal however, manna stopped falling. After circumcision and the celebration of the goodness of the Lord, God put a final stop to the supply of emergency, temporary food, to give way to the promised fruits, the real and permanent provisions. Manna was a temporary food for the Israelites in the wilderness, whether they were lazy or not, food would be available. Their sin never made manna to cease from falling. But at Gilgal, manna ceased to fall.

A baby Christian enjoys certain grace that encourages him to want to serve the Lord the more. He may not like fasting at all, yet when he prays a little sign would follow. With little or no knowledge of the word of God, his prayer and weak faith still produce result. At that stage of his Christian life he is enjoying manna, free food. His sin does not stop answer to his prayer.

However, a time is coming in his Christian journey when he will get to Gilgal. There on, the Lord will expect him to begin to fast, and pray in other to have desired results. He must have faith if he wants his prayer answered. Though in the time past, whether he had faith or not, he received surprises from God. As he moved from one man of God to another, his prayers were answered. But, from Gilgal, even if the whole saints in the world join hands together to pray for him, the situation will not change completely until he learns how to do it by moving closer to the Lord.

The aim of the Lord is to make him grow up to maturity. He too must reach a stage whereby he will receive anointing to set the captives of the mighty free. The Lord needs more workers in the field, therefore, one worker cannot be allowed to be idle or lazy, and yet live in comfort.

Many Christians have lost out in Gilgal. When they have just given their lives, things were easy, but thereafter, it looks as if the Lord is no longer listening to, or caring for them. Though they fast and pray fervently, poverty would just not depart from their lives. Until they move closer to God to know the cause of the poverty, movement from one crusade to another will not help their condition. Perhaps they do not pay the correct (full) tithe of their income, at Gilgal God will not exempt them from being attacked by devourers even though before Gilgal they were exempted. Many Christians that are lazy in their prayer life continue to suffer, the prayer of their pastors notwithstanding, until they learn to relate with God directly through His dear Son Jesus Christ, their problem may worsen. At Gilgal, a Christian must cease to be a babe in Christ, he must grow to maturity. God is not interested in a spiritual dwarf child, a child that crawls for years. A child who after many years is still unable to feed himself is a disgrace to the Father. God will therefore make sure that He teaches him how to get things done.

Sometimes in the promised-land, when the whole generation of the people that fought wars in other to possess the promised-land had all died, the Lord did one thing concerning the generations of Israelites living in the promised-land, but had no single war experience.

"These are the nations the Lord left to test all those Israelites who had not experienced any of the wars in Canaan (He did this only to teach warfare to the descendants of the Israelites who had not had previous battle experience)" (Judges 3:1-2 NIV).

Who knows, perhaps the battle in your life that has been left there for this long was left to train and make you a strong Christian. But, the earlier you understand this, the earlier the battle is fully won. We cannot afford to be lazy Christians, Jesus did not die in our stead that we might become lazy children of God. Rather the Holy Spirit is sent to us that we might become fire-brand children of God. Every Christian must have Gilgal experience. Success in Gilgal will promote us to Bethel—a stage in our Christian life when we receive clearly the revelation of the Lord. We shall move on to Jericho—where we begin to win every battle of life as heavens defend and fight for us and we get to Jordan—a realm where it becomes impossible for us to doubt God.

Waiting upon the Lord

"And kings shall be thy nursing fathers, and their queens thy nursing mothers: they shall bow down to thee with their face toward the earth, and lick up the dust of thy feet; and thou shall know that I am the Lord: for they shall not be ashamed that wait for me" (Isaiah 49:23).

Now, waiting on the Lord simply means you do only what is expected of you, playing your own role as stated in the covenant you have with the Lord, while you deliberately abandon and refuse to do what God is expected to do. Even when a thousand fall by your side, and ten thousand fall by your right hand, waiting calmly for the act of God without you going on stage to play God is "waiting on the Lord". The waiting period is the time between the crisis period and the manifestation of God's glory. Often, it's like a dark hour, when confusion seems to dominate the hour. It's the most tempting period.

King Saul had a terrible bad experience at Gilgal. May we never have such an experience in Jesus name. There at Gilgal he chose his destiny while he denied himself of the glorious plan of God. In I Samuel 10:1, Samuel the priest anointed Saul as the king of Israel, and thereafter gave Saul this instruction.

"And thou shall go down before me to Gilgal; and, behold, I will come down unto thee, to offer burnt offerings, and to sacrifice sacrifices of peace offerings: seven days shall thou tarry, till I come to thee, and show thee what thou shall do" (I Samuel 10:8).

At Gilgal, King Saul was to await Samuel for seven days. For this number of days, Saul had virtually nothing to do but to wait for Samuel. About two years later when Saul had started his reign in Israel, there arose a war between Israel and the Philistines. Then, Saul and the people went to Gilgal to wait for Samuel the priest.

"And the Philistines gather themselves together to fight with Israel, thirty thousand chariots, and six thousand horsemen, and people as the sand which is on the sea shore in multitude: and they came up, and pitched in Michmash, eastward from Beth-aven". I Samuel 13:5.

Here, the Philistines were fully prepared for war. The number of the men of war of Philistines made the Israelites to tremble. When the Israelites saw that their situation was critical and that their army was had pressed, they all scattered, they hid themselves in caves, thickets, among rocks, some of them even hid in pits and cisterns (that is, inside wells!) For some other Israelites, the fear of the calamity that might befall them made them to flee from Jerusalem. They crossed the Jordan to the land of Gad and Gilead. The Bible let us know in I Samuel 14:21, that some Israelites even fled to the Philistines to join them! That tells you the level of their fear. They had no confidence in the Israeli army, and because of that they went to the camp of the enemies to surrender. Yes, they walked to the camp of the enemies to surrender their lives. Perhaps, worst of all, only Saul and his son Jonathan had swords among the whole army of Israel (I Samuel 13:22). Really, it was a terrible situation.

"Saul remained at Gilgal, and all the troops with him were quaking with fear. He waited seven days, the time set by Samuel; but Samuel did not come to Gilgal, and Saul's men began to scatter" (I Samuel 13:7-8).

After he had been anointed, Samuel had told him to wait for him at Gilgal for seven days, that he might come to show Saul what Saul should do. Now the enemies had come, hard pressed against the army of Israel. Seven days had come, yet Samuel did not show up.

At Gilgal, there the Lord renews the strength of the people that wait for Him. But, since we cannot predict precisely when the Lord will come, waiting seems boring. As we wait for God on something, we should not expect people around us to encourage us. Are you waiting upon the Lord for the blessing of the womb? Do not expect your relations to encourage you, it will be a great surprise if your in-laws do not discourage and try to frustrate your faith. But, it is only you that the Lord has called. He has no business with the people around you. As you wait upon the Lord, God watches over one person, it is you. It is only you that understand that you must wait for the Lord; if and only if there will be complete victory.

Gilgal is a place to wait for the Lord without wavering. A place where the child of God must not lose hope, he must hold on to his hope, making his hope ever alive that God may establish such a person for ever. In your family, working place, even in the church, no other person understands the reason you must keep on waiting and not go for the alternative. At Gilgal, people that you trust will mock and desert you, yet you must wait on the Lord. When Jesus needed the support of His disciples most, that was when they could not control their sleep. Imagine, the Lord had never asked them for any help before, just this time alone He wanted them to join hand with Him in prayer, they just kept on sleeping even when He came to rebuke them, they still would not support Him. When Job had no one to turn to other than his wife, she told him to curse the Lord and just die. Job desired to live more, but his wife was fed up, to her, death was better than hoping in the Lord. Since Job loved life he chose to trust more in the Lord. However, with Saul, that was not the case.

Before we begin to blame Saul we need to grab the understanding of the condition he was facing. When we succeed in this, then it will help us to overcome the same situation where he fell. For this is where King Saul failed and made him not to be among the legends of the Lord. For instance, Saul had only three thousand soldiers to fight against the Philistines that numbered close to five hundred thousand well equipped soldiers. 3,000 soldiers against about 500,000 well equipped soldiers. That was the first calamity. The second is that, the soldiers of Israel deserted Saul, out of the three thousand soldiers, only six hundred remained with Saul. Eighty per cent of his soldiers had fled. It's like you had ten people supporting you against many oppositions, and then suddenly, you looked back to see your supporters, rather than seeing ten you saw only two! It is frustrating!

"And Saul said, Bring hither a burnt offering to me, and peace offerings. And he offered the burnt offering.

And it came to pass, that as soon as he had made an end of offering, behold, Samuel came: and Saul went out to meet him, that he might salute him".

The fear of the havoc the enemies could cause made Saul to perform the duty of Samuel the priest. Just like most of us, when the coming of the Lord seemed delayed, we go on stage to play the role expected of the Lord. It could be that you need a wife, and you bring the lady that you have found to the Lord in prayer. You waited for an answer from the Lord, but the Lord seemed not to be speaking, as many would do, you just take the silence of God to mean His approval. You may be a lady looking for a husband. You live a descent and godly life. However, that type of life seems not to attract any man to you. You have prayed for the right man to come, yet he is no where to be found and you are getting older everyday. People keep telling you; "Find something doing, you are a lady, you may soon reach menopause" As a result of such pressure, you just change friends, from godly friends to worldly friends, so that you can get a man. What you are saying is, "At least, if God does not know how to get me a man, I can find one for myself". For some of us, God promised us that we would travel abroad, for instance Europe, and somehow, time keeps rolling by and the promise seemed far from being fulfilled, we just get on stage to play God. There on the stage, we chose when, how and where to travel to. Many of us Christians in a bid to prosper, we wait on the Lord, but it was like, the longer we wait, the poorer the situations become. Then, we go on the stage to play God. We get involved in fraudulent activities, illicit businesses. We do these because we think "What if God is not coming?" But the truth is, if it is a good thing, God will surely come just as Samuel came to Saul on the same seventh day. God will not delay your blessings a day longer than when it is appointed to come.

"And Samuel said to Saul, Thou hast done foolishly: thou hast not kept the commandment of the Lord thy God, which He commanded thee: for now would the Lord have established thy kingdom upon Israel for ever" (I Samuel 13:13)

So, the plan of the Lord was to establish the kingdom of Saul for ever and Saul was not aware of God's plan when he was waiting for Samuel. So, there was a purpose for the "delay", it was to give Saul opportunity before the Lord to be considered as a man whose dynasty would be forever in Israel. That was the plan on the mind of God. But Saul must first be proved. Saul would have got what David later got! But he could not wait. With God, delay is not denial. Many are Christians that the Lord had purposed to elevate, He wants them to be the head in all spiritual matters, He would have blessed some people with abundant wealth and overflowing anointing. But such people had allowed the pressure from friends, relations, colleagues, the enemies and the so called life problems and challenges to make them lose hope in the Lord. They therefore miss their glorious destiny.

They that wait upon the Lord at Gilgal are established for ever, but they that stop waiting are overthrown by the Lord. Please take a time out and meditate on what the word of the Lord has to say on waiting on the Lord.

"Wait on the Lord: be of good courage, and He shall strengthen thine heart: wait; I say wait on the Lord" (Psalm 27:14).

"Rest in the Lord and wait patiently for Him: fret not thyself because of him who prospereth in his way, because of the man who bringeth wicked devices to pass.

For evil doers shall be cut off! But those that wait upon the Lord, they shall inherit the earth. Wait on the Lord and keep His way, and He shall exalt thee to inherit the land: when the wicked are cut off, thou shall see it" (Psalm 37:7, 9, and 34).

Do not be pushed around by anything called problem, you should rather push problem out of the way. Even if heaven will fall while waiting for the Lord, please wait for Him, for no one that waits for Him is ever put to shame. Let the enemies roar like lion, do not fear them for you have the original Lion, the Lion of Judah. If while waiting for the faithfulness of the Lord death threatens. Do not stop to wait, for He that you are waiting for is the only One that swallowed death in victory. Then, if He that swallowed death in victory lives in you, death has no power over you. If while waiting, losses and defeat try to raise their ugly heads, still do not throw into the sea your precious hope. All that the enemies are waiting for is to see you lose your hope, so that you can be disconnected from the Almighty God, your Defender.

"Now faith is the substance of things hoped for, the evidence of things not seen. But without faith it is impossible to please Him" (Hebrews 11:1, 6).

In faith there is hope, for faith is the assurance of the things hoped for. Faith is impotent and is crippled whenever hope is lost. For faith to work greatly, hope must be alive. Whenever the enemies threaten, it is not that they attempt to destroy you for they know that they cannot touch you. Rather, their threat is only meant to make you lose your hope in the Lord, they plan to exterminate your hope, so that your faith can be crippled, unable to produce desired result. And we know that without faith no one can please God.

Every Christian has Gilgal experience. All the great men and women of God performing signs and wonders worldwide have at one time or the other had their own experience at Gilgal. No one can go to Bethel, Jericho and/or Jordan without first returning from Gilgal. Many Christians avoid Gilgal, they are not circumcised in their heart, they remain babes in Christ, and can not wait upon the Lord without losing their hope. Yet, they pray for great revelation, they want the Lord to fight the battles in their lives, they desire great faith that wrought signs and wonders. The Lord will not raise a man who will but fall in Gilgal to replace His legend. The man that easily turns to man of flesh for help when the help from the Lord seems not forthcoming can not be a vessel of honour. Before going to the next section, permit me to say this; God is a giver of second chance. If you have missed it and you are humble enough to come to God, by confessing your sin and asking for forgiveness, God will surely forgive and forget your sin. He will wash you in the blood and give you a new beginning.

"If we confess our sins, He is faithful and just to forgive our sins, and to cleanse us from all unrighteousness" (1 John 1:9).

Waiting Successfully

It is needful to discuss how to wait successfully for the Lord. If failure in Gilgal will hinder us from reaching Bethel, Jericho and Jordan, then we must pray fervently to the Lord to show us the way to succeed in Gilgal. And then ask for sufficient grace to be obedient and accept His word, His way.

"I beseech you therefore, brethren, by the mercies of God, that ye present your bodies a living sacrifice, holy, acceptable unto God, which is your reasonable service". Romans 12:1

The above scripture is the key to waiting upon the Lord. Here, the Holy Spirit through Paul begged us by the abundant mercies of God that we present, offer our bodies as living sacrifice, holy and acceptable to God. Animals sacrificed to God in the Old Testament days suffered death. The priests would separate the parts and would do with the sacrifice according to the commandment of the Lord. Animals that were sacrificed suffered death. But ours is different, as we offer our bodies as sacrifice to God, we remain alive. God does not need our bodies as sacrifice when we are dead, it must be when we are alive. Your body starts from the crown of your head to the sole of your feet: your head, the hair on your head, your eyes, nose, ears, mouth, down to your heart. Your hands, legs, your life, everything that is found in this tabernacle called body. Everything that makes up a man is found in the body.

A sacrifice that is offered to God belongs to God, the worshipper that offers it has nothing to do with what God does with the sacrifice. If God likes, He may instruct the priests to burn it, roast it in fire or cook it. Sometimes, the priests burn part of it and boil the rest as food. It is an exclusive right of God to determine and dictate what to do with the sacrifice offered. It is only when God has done freely what He wants to do with the sacrifice that the giver of the sacrifice can be blessed. When you offer sacrifice to the Lord, you leave Him to handle it the way He think best, for He alone owns it.

As we now offer our bodies to God as a living sacrifice, then, nothing concerns us on what God does with our bodies. We need not be anxious on what to eat because the body we want to feed is no more ours, it belongs to God. We must not commit sin because we want to feed this body with good food. We should not be concerned to the extent that we commit sin as we cloth this body and decorate it with ornament, and gold. If someone rises up to kill this body, we do not need to fear death to the extent of losing hope in God, after all, it is no longer ours, let us see if He will allow man to destroy His belongings. If someone insults me, that should not make me to respond by saying; "You are a fool!" For then I shall be in danger of hell fire (Matthew 5:22). Whoever wishes may insult me, for I am no more mine, my body is the temple of the Holy Spirit. That person had only insulted the temple of the Lord. And what you do to the temple, you do to the Spirit that dwells there. When a man slaps my right cheek, I can confidently turn the left to him in accordance with the word of the Lord. The man had not really slapped me, but he had defiled the temple of the Lord. When a man cheats me, I do not need to repay evil with evil, the person has only treated with contempt the sacrifice of the Lord. The two children of Eli-the priest of God that did it died young, they never saw their next generation and their family became ruined suddenly.

It becomes the duty of the Lord to take care of our bodies once we have offered them as living sacrifice to God. He Himself will fight for us and defend us. God will become our Shepherd and provide for all our needs. But before He can do this, we must sincerely offer our bodies to Him as living sacrifice. They that are sick, barren, sisters and brothers with delayed marriage, those under the oppression of the enemies, among others, need not lose hope in their God. Let them offer first their bodies to God as a living sacrifice, and then they will see if the Lord will allow any demon, enemy or devil to glory over such bodies. No demon of sickness can dwell in the body that belongs to God, neither will He allow any demon of barrenness to dwell in such body, hence all the people of God that were barren in the Bible had glorious children. This is what it means to first seek the kingdom of God and its righteousness, and then, all other things shall be added to you. Only when we have sincerely offered our bodies to God as living sacrifice can we say like the three Hebrews in the face of death;

"If it be so, our God whom we serve is able to deliver us from the burning fiery furnace, and he will deliver us out of thine hand, O king. But if not, be it known unto thee, O king, that we will not serve thy gods, nor worship the golden image which thou hast set up" (Daniel 3:17,18).

The three Hebrew men believed that God would deliver them from the fire. However, they also assumed that God might chose not to deliver them. It was not as if they had sinned or God was wicked. They thought God might have appointed them to die for His name even as Stephen, so they were ready to be the martyrs of the Lord. If God wanted them to die for any reason, they were ready to die. They therefore told the king, that if God would not deliver them, they still would not have any regret, so, they would still not bow. The king became angry and gave instruction that the fire be increased seven fold. He really wanted to destroy these men to their bones. Of course, they were thrown into the fire. But the Lord God is a Consuming Fire, He went into the fire of the king ahead of the three Hebrew men, he consumed the fire of the king. Therefore, the fire being seeing by the people was no more the fire of the king, but the Lord-the Consuming Fire. When the three Hebrew men were thrown into the fire, they were not hurt for it was like being in the Lord. The Lord welcomes them. But, for the men that threw them into the fire, they died instantly as a result of the heat of the Consuming fire. Everything that was of the enemy in the bodies of the Hebrew men got burnt into ashes—the rope with which they were bound. When they saw the miracle, they began to worship and praise the Lord. A great fellowship service was going on in the fire! The men were rejoicing, their joy knew no bound. Then, the Lord opened the eyes of the king to see the work of the King of kings. The king was astonished. Then he called them out of the fire, shouting at the top of his voice. He did not dare to go closer to the fire, for then he too would die.

"Then the king promoted Shadrach, Meshach, and Abednego, in the province of Babylon" (Daniel 3:30).

"And therefore will the Lord wait, that He may be gracious unto you, and therefore will He be exalted, that He may have mercy upon you: for the Lord is a God of judgment: blessed are all they that wait for Him" (Isaiah 30:18).

"And kings shall be thy nursing fathers, and their queens thy nursing mothers: they shall bow down to thee with their face toward the earth, and lick up the dust of thy feet: and thou shall know that I am the Lord: for they shall not be ashamed that wait for me" (Isaiah 49:23).

Chapter Five
Overcoming the Destroyers of Destiny

Man's destiny at the beginning

Every man created by God on this planet earth has a glorious, beautiful destiny. The first man Adam was created to be fruitful, to multiply, replenish the earth, subdue it and have dominion. That first purpose for creating man still remains His purpose for every man that comes to God through Jesus. Yes, we can say that the devil had destroyed that destiny of man. He had succeeded in robbing man of God-given glory. That the first Adam fell before the devil, his falling therefore makes every man a captive of the devil.

Our God is a good God, kind and merciful. Knowing that the fall of the first Adam meant the fall of his future generations, God therefore sent the last Adam—the Lord Jesus Christ. Our first birth into this world was through the first Adam, now for remedy to be done in the life of man, God sent the Lord Jesus, as the last Adam.

Through Jesus, we receive another birth called the new birth. We become born-again. Christianity without new birth is a vain religion. When you are born-again, you are born again into the basic purpose of God for creating man as written in Genesis 1:26.

"And God said, Let us make man in our image, after our likeness: and let them have dominion over the sea, and over the fowl of the air, and over the cattle, and over all the earth, and over every creeping thing that creepeth upon the earth".

If our first birth were enough to usher us into our glorious destiny, there would not have been any need to go through the second birth. But, the devil has power and dominion over every man that remains in the first birth. Jesus needed not come into this world to suffer if His coming would make no difference in the life of man. But thank God that Jesus our last Adam came. His coming launches us into the glorious will of God. Thus, His coming confirms Job 9:4.

"He (God) is wise in heart, and mighty in strength: who hath hardened himself against Him, and hath prospered?"

God is the creator of wisdom. The devil couldn't have had wisdom if God had not given him. God, the giver of wisdom is therefore wiser than the devil. The Lord showed the supremacy of His will by sending Jesus into this world to give us a new beginning that will afford us to have a glorious ending. When you become born-again, you are born again into the divine will of God. Your new birth means that you are born into the family of God.

"But as many as received Him, to them gave He power to become the sons of God, even to them that believe on His name: which were born not of blood, nor of the will of the flesh, nor of the will of man, but of God" (John 1:12,13).

It is of the will of our parents that we were born into this world, and that birth made us to inherit the nature of the first Adam. But our second birth is of the will of God hence, we become the children of God through which we inherit the nature of God. Thus, by the second birth we become partakers of the nature of God. Your new birth gives you access to the riches and wealth of God. You become the determinant of your destiny, for you have the grace to ask whatever you want. Everything is made possible for you if only you will believe. Your new birth gives you the grace to put on the whole armour of God, so that the evil one has no access to your life. The blood of Jesus is made available for you to cancel every curse and nullify every written code of the enemy. God gives you the name of His dear Son, the name of Jesus, so that you wage war against the devil on the ticket of Jesus, even in His name. You are given the right to have expectation, what you want your tomorrow to be, and God gives you assurance in His word that your expectation shall not be cut off. Your new birth launches you into victorious living, never to taste defeat again. To crown it all, as you depart from this world, you have a home made ready for you in heaven, home built not by man but by God! That is the essence of our new birth, to have life, not an ordinary common life, but abundant life.

Enemy at the door!

However, there are destroyers of destiny that we have to withstand. They have no power, they are only cunning. They can never force us to do anything. Rather they offer us counsel, advice. The devil is the arch enemy of our destiny. He will try all he can to destroy our destiny by misleading us to act against our destiny. The devil in this mission is assisted by various and numerous demons.

The first Adam was made to act against his destiny by the devil when he advised Eve to eat the forbidden fruit. Mind you, the devil never forced Eve to eat it, rather, he counselled her, and then, Eve focused her attention on the forbidden fruit.

"And when the woman saw that the tree was good for food, and that it was pleasant to the eyes, and a tree to be desired to make one wise, she took of the fruit thereof, and did eat, and gave also her husband with her; and he did eat" (Genesis 3:6).

After the counsel of the devil, Eve looked and fixed her eyes on the tree. As she was looking, in her heart she thought and concluded that the tree would make her wise, hence, she desired the fruit. After she desired it, she stretched forth her hand, plucked the fruit and ate it. The devil did not force Eve's eyes on the tree, neither did he make her heart to ponder on the fruit nor force her hand to pluck it. Instead, the counsel of the devil made Eve to take those three steps that took her far away from her glorious destiny. One of the greatest things that the devil and his falling angels can do to destroy the destiny of man is to fire sinful thoughts into the heart of man, to hinder man's success. They tend to make things difficult and unbearable. But a man of vision will not give in, he will remain focused.

Truly, God had told Elijah to go and anoint Elisha as the new prophet. God had purposed it, but Elisha had to contend with the enemies of his destiny. If you do not have a glorious destiny, then the destroyers of destiny have nothing against you. The madman on the street has little or no enemies. Though he eats unhygienic food, the demons of dysentery and cholera never see him, they themselves would flee from him. The demon of suicide considered it foolish to move the madman to take his life, for there is nothing glorious to snatch away from this madman. There is no good thing in his life therefore there is no reason for battles.

However, for every man with glorious destiny, there are battles to confront. The man needs to withstand and overcome these destroyers of destiny before he can ever enter into his destiny. Even our Lord Jesus Christ once contended with them. After he had fasted for forty days and forty nights, in preparation for the work of the ministry He was about to start. Just when the fasting and prayer had ended, when he was shouting Hallelujah: having the assurance that now He had the support of the whole heavens to go ahead in the work. Just then the destroyer of destiny came to Him.

The devil remembered how he made the first Adam to fall: it was through food therefore, the first temptation he brought to the last Adam was on food. To him, every Adam loves food and would not mind what it would take to keep body and soul together. He advised Jesus to turn stones to bread. Though Jesus was hungry, He would rather agree to die of hunger than to obey the voice of the devil. The last temptation according to St. Matthew was to offer Jesus the kingdoms of the world, if only Jesus would worship him. Despite that offer, Jesus refused to worship the creature rather than the Creator. The devil took time out to tempt Jesus in all ways, simply because he knew that Jesus had a glorious destiny. You and I also have to contend with these destroyers of destiny for us to achieve our destiny. Every one that runs to avoid the destroyers of destiny runs far away from his glorious destiny. Thank God that Jesus had conquered every destroyer of destiny on our behalf. It would have been impossible for any man to overcome them if Jesus had not defeated them for our sakes.

Someone would now say, "Why do I still contend with them?" But remember that every one that is born into this world is created to subdue and exercise dominion. The word *subdue* according to Oxford Dictionary of current English means to conquer, subjugate or tame. If there is no struggle or battle, there will be no reason to subdue. Only in the coming New Jerusalem and in the New Heaven there shall be no war. However, remember that our new birth ushers us back into the initial purpose of God for creating man. But in the present time, we do not fight the battle by our own power and might. The truth is, in the spirit realm, we do not fight any battle, for we fight in the name of Jesus. That is, we fight in His name, on His behalf, on His ticket. If we were to fight in our own names, we shall be conquered by the devil. But we fight in the name of Jesus, who the Bible says He is the head of all principality and powers. We fight in the name of Jesus who had conquered the devil. It becomes impossible that we be defeated. Our appearance in the battle field is to claim and receive our victory. We go to the battle to have a walk-over over the enemy.

Person of the destroyers of destiny.

The destroyers of destiny, really, are not the people that we see in the physical realm. Though men can be used, they are not the real person, they are mere vessels.

"For we wrestle not against flesh and blood, but against principalities, and against powers, against the rulers of the darkness of this world, against spiritual wickedness in high places" (Ephesians 6:12).

God commanded Elijah;

"Elisha the son of Shaphat of Abelmeholah shalt thou anoit to be

prophet in thy room" (I Kings 19:16).

Elijah was obedient to the commandment of the Lord.

"So he (Elijah) *departed thence, and found Elisha the son of Shaphat, who was plowing with twelve yoke of oxen before him, and he with the twelveth: and Elijah passed by him, and cast his mantle upon him. And he* (Elisha) *arose, and went after Elijah, and ministered unto him"* (I Kings 19:19-21).

Elijah was faithful in the assignment by casting his mantle on Elisha. Immediately Elijah's mantle fell on Elisha, Elisha got the message that he was to collect baton from Elijah. So, Elisha too was obedient to the call by following Elijah immediately. As it is, the destroyers of destiny always come when our obedience is full, when the battle is indeed over. Just as the Lord had received the fullness of the Holy Spirit, He had fasted and prayed for forty days and forty nights. He had had enough time to fellowship with the Father, even to study the scriptures. It was after all these that the devil came to tempt Him. Now we understand God's word in I Corinthians 10:13.

"There hath no temptation taken you but such as is common to man: but God is faithful, who will not suffer you to be tempted above that ye are able; but will with the temptation also make a way to escape, that ye may be able to bear it".

Likewise for Elisha, he had already become the friend of God through his obedience to the call to service. Elisha had also spent some years with Elijah to acquire knowledge and get to know the Lord more before the destroyers of destiny showed up before him. If the destroyers of destiny dare come against you, do not fret, know that they have come at the appropriate time when you shall be victorious.

Now when the time was ripe for Elisha to step fully into his destiny, the sons of the prophets came to him.

The Operation of the destroyers of destiny

"And the sons of the prophets that were at bethel came forth to Elisha, and said unto him, Knowest thou that the Lord will take away thy master from thy hand to day?" 2 Kings 2:3.

Focus on imminent loss

These so called the sons of the prophets had been in the prophet-hood training before Elisha, thus, they could be considered to having more experience than Elisha. They came to tell him that his master Elijah would be taken from Elisha that day. They focused the mind of Elisha on what he would lose. Of course, Elijah the great prophet would be taken away that very day, Elisha would never on earth set his eyes on Elijah again. These prophets in-training called the sons of prophet were vessels used by the devil against Elisha, just as Peter was used by the devil against Jesus (Read Matthew 16:21-23). There, Peter spoke sternly against the destiny of Jesus, so also the sons of the prophet.

When you are about to take a giant step to progress in life, and a spirit focuses your attention on the immediate or imminent problems without offering holy solution to it, that spirit is a destroyer of destiny. No matter the magnitude of the problem, if a spirit would keep telling you that your end has come, that must be a destroyer of destiny. The sons of the prophet were like telling Elisha; "Now, your master and lord will be taken away from you today, you will be left alone. You are a young prophet in training for about five years, how would you now cope without Elijah? You are happy to collect baton from the hand of Elijah. That is good. But you know that you have no power. How then would you live the rest of your life?" Whatever spirit that keeps telling you in the face of problems that "You should have in the time past done this and that" That is a destroyer of destiny. Holy Spirit of the Living God will never do that. He will not focus your attention on the problem, rather on the solution. The Holy Spirit is a carrier of solution, but the devil and his demons are carriers and revealers of problems.

Focus on limitation and weakness

These destroyers of destiny are cunning. They keep sending evil thoughts into our hearts, though we do not easily know that such thoughts are from the evil one. While you are organising a programme to bless the body of Christ and God's kingdom, sometimes while you have just finished saying a special prayer, the spirit might whisper "*You should have done it this way, that would have granted you great success*" That is a destroyer of destiny. The sons of the prophet told Elisha, "Your master will be taken from you today, you lack power, yet you can not go back into farming, your former profession. Perhaps, you should not have burnt all your oxen and farm equipment. Oh! There is danger ahead of you". They could not tell him the blessing Elisha would receive as a result of Elijah's departure. Rather, they were telling him his past wrong decision taken. God is enough to make up for our past shortcomings. That which you left undone yesterday was known to God some centuries before you were born. God knew you would make that mistake even before you were born. God is not acting on our behalf at the time we begin to pray. Prior to the time we discover a problem and start praying, many centuries before then, God knew about it and He also knew how you would react to it and what your prayer would be. God is abundantly able to make up for our shortcomings. Our prayer only ushers us into what God has provided for us. Before the devil came to sift Peter, Jesus had prayed for Peter. The Scriptures did not tell us precisely when Jesus prayed for Peter, but the important thing is that before Peter's days of tribulation, Jesus had prayed for him.

The Lord has said; "*Ask, and it shall be given you*" (Matthew 7:7).

There is already provision for whatever we shall ask for. "*Not by might, nor by power, but by my Spirit, saith the Lord of hosts*" (Zechariah 4:6).

Are you weak such that a spirit begins to condemn you and prophesy that you can not achieve much as a result of your weakness? I tell you without mincing word that, that is a destroyer of destiny. The purpose of that spirit is to make you accept failure. They want you to agree and believe that your weakness automatically means failure. But what saith the Lord concerning our weakness?

"*My grace is sufficient for thee: for my strength is made perfect in weakness*" (2 Corinthians 12:9). When Apostle Paul heard this word from the Lord, then he said; "*Therefore I take pleasure in infirmities, in reproaches, in necessities, in persecutions, in distresses for Christ's sake: for when I am weak, then I am strong*" (2 Corinthians 12:10).

"For with God nothing shall be impossible" (Luke 1:37).

Is it only with the Lord that nothing shall be impossible? Certainly not. Jesus said to one man that came to Him for help;

"... If thou canst believe, all things are possible to him that believeth" (Mark 9:23).

But the mission of the destroyers of destiny is to make us think, to confess and accept that certain things are not possible, especially things that pertain to our destiny. The truth is, with God all things are possible, and with us the children of God, the believers, all things are possible. If only we will believe, Jesus said that all things are possible to him that believes. Thus, faith transfers us from the realm of man to divine realm, being children of God; we manifest the character of God. Our faith in Him makes all things possible. If you can take it, faith makes us to operate in the class of God! Therefore, whether we do it as expected or not, it is no barrier to our success. Think of Elisha, he knew little about prayer, remember he was a farmer by profession, a mechanized farmer. When Elijah asked him;

"Ask what I shall do for thee, before I be taken away from thee. And Elisha said, I pray thee, let a double portion of thy spirit be upon me" (2 Kings 2:9).

A Bible student of today will not ask for the double portion of the spirit of his pastor, because the pastor does not perform all the signs and wonders through his own human spirit, but through the Spirit of the Lord upon the pastor. Despite this, the Lord answered Elisha with the right answer. Here, wrong request notwithstanding brought the right answer. God deals with our heart not our brain. He wants our trust and confidence to be on Him, nor in our ability.

Use of Distractions and discouragement

The sons of the prophet came to Elisha at Bethel to discourage him and lead him away from his glorious destiny. When he and Elijah left Bethel for Jericho, another set of sons of the prophet came to him also with the purpose of discouraging him. Even when Elisha refused to be discouraged, another fifty men of the sons of the prophet followed Elisha and Elijah and stood afar off to watch these two men of God.

One thing should be noted here, at every location specially arranged by the Lord for the promotion of Elisha-Bethel—a period in his life when he was to receive anointing for revelation, Jericho—when he was to receive anointing for victory and breakthrough and then Jordan – when God had a plan to enrich the faith of Elisha, at all these periods in time—these destroyers of destiny appeared to Elisha to distract him from the plans and purpose of the Lord. That is to say, at every level or stage that God has designed for our promotion, during specially arranged activities or events which God has appointed for our uplift, the devil and his agents are set to bring distraction and discouragement.

When the Lord gives us divine visitation either to give us great revelation from His word, to reveal a secret to us, or to grant us knowledge, these destroyers of destiny always creep in to flash some thoughts into our mind to create distractions. It could be when you are listening to a sermon, at the point where you would be blessed most, just then you remember an issue that once happened at home or in your place of work. At times when it has been ordained that you receive great revelation as you study your Bible, or when in the spirit realm you need to pray most, just then you feel tired, and would want to reduce the time you will spend in the presence of the Lord. Sometimes, when a sermon is going on in the Church, when heaven had programmed you for breakthrough, then, a friend may want to engage you in some issue that has nothing good to add to your life.

How to overcome the destroyers of destiny
Refuse to dialogue with them
Something made Elisha to overcome these destroyers of destiny. When the sons of the prophet would tell him; *'Do you know that Elijah your master will be taken from you today?'* Elisha would reply them;

"Yea, I know it, hold ye your peace" (2 Kings 2:3,5).

Elisha would cut the discussion short abruptly. He never gave them room for discussion, as he had no time to engage in dialogue with them. It was like saying, "Yes, I know but you keep your mouth shut!" Elisha would tell them. Every Christian that will fulfil destiny must avoid dialogue with the devil and his agents. If such a Christian must dialogue with any spirit at all, it must be with the Holy Spirit. Ordinarily, when the dialogue begins, it will be as if you are just meditating in your heart. Brethren, if the meditation is unbiblical, if it will not help your faith in Christ, if it will lead you away from success, then, you have just been visited by a destroyer of destiny.

To cut short discussions with these enemies of our destiny demands that we get acquainted with the word of God. Or else, how will you test the spirit that is conversing with you whether it is of the Lord or not? Jesus applied this principle when the devil came to tempt Him. The devil knew that Jesus had a glorious destiny, he also knew that Jesus had come into the world to overthrow him.

"Again, the devil taketh him up into an exceeding high mountain, and sheweth Him all the kingdoms of the world, and the glory of them,

And saith unto Him, All these things will I give thee, if thou wilt fall down and worship me" (Matthew 4:8, 9).

The devil is wise and cunning. He did not want Jesus to wait till God would place everything under the feet of Jesus. The devil promised to give them all to Jesus if only Jesus would worship him the devil. The destiny of Jesus was not just to have all power on earth, but also in heaven too. The destiny of Jesus was to have a name that would be highly honoured in heaven, on earth and in hell. But the destroyer of destiny offered Jesus just one out of the three. Though he would give the earth to Jesus, excluding his very self, so that he could at the end be the lord over Jesus. Immediately the devil got to that point;

"Then saith Jesus unto him, Get thee hence, Satan: for it is written, Thou shall worship the Lord thy God, and Him only shalt thou serve.

Then the devil leaveth Him, and, behold, angels came and ministered unto Him" (Matthew 4:10-11).

Jesus cut the devil shut and rebuked him by casting him out. Understand this, until Jesus shut the door of His heart against the devil, Satan never left. And then, until the devil left Him the angels did not come to minister to Him. The inability of Eve to cut short the discussion between her and the devil made her to lose destiny for life. Never allow the destroyers of destiny to have time to achieve their purpose in your life. The moment you recognize them, cast them out!

Reject "half-bread is better than none" syndrome

In the third temptation brought before Jesus as recorded by Saint Matthew, the destroyer of destiny was actually telling Jesus to settle for less, "that half bread is better than none". The devil seemed to be saying; "You do not need to labour at all, here is success at ease. Right here on the mountain you have what you have been praying for. You may not need to go to the cross at Calvary to suffer, this is cheap. Take this half bread, at least for now. Be satisfied with this little achievement, for many people have tried to get it before you but they all failed. You are fortunate, take it, be satisfied, after all, this achievement still places you far above your colleagues". Whatever spirit that tells you to settle for anything less than your destiny is a destroyer of destiny. In Christ you can do all things, not many things but all things.

Many pastors that would have become very great have had their destinies destroyed by the devil. The destroyers of destiny make them to compare themselves with fellow pastors around them, especially within the same church, denomination or locality. Then, they quickly notice that they are more anointed than others, therefore, they are satisfied with the level of their anointing and achievement. Perhaps, they discovered that they have the largest congregation, then, they tend to relax, they have little or no interest in effective soul-winning activities again. It could be that in the presence of many people, your pastor praised you for your dedication and for many great things the Lord has been doing through you. As a result of this, you feel fulfilled.

Many men of God are fervent in prayer, and in the study of the word. They sanctified themselves that they might be vessels of honour in the hand of the Lord. But, just when they begin to notice the manifestation of some spiritual gifts in their lives, though, the Lord had just started demonstrating His power through them. The destroyers of destiny make them think they too have now arrived, that they have made it. Just immediately they accept such suicidal belief, their success is pegged. Before they know it, the rate of their fasting and prayer begins to dwindle. Unless they identify the cause of their falling, no matter how much they struggle to get up, the struggle will be in vain. If you want to walk your way to the class of the legend, you must not buy this lie of the devil.

That the devil might not have undue advantage over us, the Lord Jesus gave us a standard we should reach before we begin to get satisfied with our achievements.

"Verily, verily, I say unto you, He that believeth on me, the works that I do shall he do also; and greater works than these shall he do; because I go unto my Father" (John 14:12).

Our destinies as God's children are not negotiable, we must therefore not settle for anything less. Every Christian is given a glorious destiny, to perform greater works than the Lord. Irrespective of when we believe, whether at young or old age, there is a sufficient grace to sustain us all.

Chapter Six
A man of vision

Why vision?

As it is, God has no pleasure in a vision-less person. The reason being that if God should give such a person a high calling, lack of vision will limit the scope and the operation of such a person. So many people in the work of the ministry are indeed called and anointed by the Holy Spirit, they have the anointing to become spiritual giants. Unfortunately, they remain spiritual dwarfs! God is not happy with a man that lacks vision for his life and the ministry. Before He created man for instance, He had the vision of His desire clearly, that the man He would create would be the greatest among all the works of His hand. Therefore, man shall be made after the likeness and in the image of God. If then man has both the likeness and the image of God, then he must have dominion over everything on earth, he should be empowered to subdue the earth. If God is great, then, the only creature created in the likeness and image of God must be great. That is the more reason the word of God says man shall judge the angels on the judgment day (I Corinthians 6:2,3). The vision of God concerning His creatures guided Him to create things that were good in His sight.

The vision here is not prophecy, neither is it the vision of the night when you dream in your sleep, nor what is revealed to us. Rather, the vision here is having the mental picture of what you desire the future to be. This vision is an imaginative insight into the future. Setting a goal to be achieved, knowing today what the life achievement will be tomorrow. Vision is painting, designing your tomorrow for your heart to see today. In other words, vision is seeing the final product even before the start of the production of the product. Vision is that discovery of God's purpose for your life. This is what makes a vision different from fantasies. Fantasy is far-fetched idea, imagination unrestricted by reality, a daydream. Fantasy emanates from the flesh, but vision has its source from the Lord. A man that receives anointing without vision is like a blind man sent on a glorious mission without an aid. No matter how glorious the mission is, or how zealous the man may be to succeed in the mission; the blind man will miss his way, unless he is guided by an aid. The vision is the destination, the final goal, while the mission is the way to reaching the destination. When you do not know where you are going, you will end up where you are not going. Now, if God gives a man a powerful anointing, yet the man has no vision, that is, he lacks specific destination, he will be easily distracted, whatever good thing that comes his way, he will accept, even when such good thing has no glorious ending.

Be focused

"All things are lawful for me, but all things are not expedient: all things are lawful for me, but all things edify not" (I Corinthians 10:23).

It is the vision a man has that pushes him to pursue a goal restlessly, even when everyone around him does not believe in his pursuit. For such a person, he is fully convinced that it is possible to achieve his goal, not only that, he also has in his mind the picture of what the success would be like and what it would bring. Since he is the only one that sees the vision, to every one around him, he is an unserious person. For instance, Watson was in the laboratory carrying out many tests on how to invent bulb. After thousands of failed tests, knowing the fact that a single test consumes time, money and energy, still Watson did not give up even after over a thousand tests had been carried out. Many of his colleagues would have thought, "Is it compulsory that we produce bulb? Isn't there any other human needs? If bulb can't be produced now, why not try some other things?" But Watson had no other vision on human need other than the invention of bulb. He eventually succeeded, and that immortalized his name till today. Vision keeps you focused.

There are many people in the Church today that live their lives without vision. Many indeed have visions, but what they spend their time, energy and resources on are things that have no meaningful contribution to helping them fulfil their vision. From childhood, our children need to be taught to remain focus and not give up easily on being the best. The above scripture in New International Version reads;

"Everything is permissible" – but not everything is beneficial. "Everything is permissible" – but not everything is constructive."

A man of vision allows his vision to guide him in his mission. God certainly saw in Elisha what He could not find in the other prophets, saints and the sons of prophet. Elisha was a man of vision, he knew how resourceful God is, even as he also knew that the decision a man takes today has a great effect in shaping his tomorrow. As a man thinks so he is. What makes a man is from the inside of man, not from the outside. Your enemies, all of them put together and the devil are not enough to make your life what it is now or what it will be tomorrow. What makes your life is what is on your inside.

"For as he thinketh in his heart, so is he…" (Proverbs 23:7).

When you keep thinking about the threatening words of the enemy, fear will certainly grip you. You cannot keep thinking failure and still expect success. When your thoughts are in agreement with the word of faith that you speak, I tell you the truth, you are not far from your joy.

When the Lord had finished His instruction to Elijah, the

scripture says;

"So he (Elijah) departed thence, and found Elisha the son of Shaphat, who was plowing with twelve yoke of oxen before him, and he with the twelfth" (I Kings 19:19).

The above scriptural verse shows that Elisha was a farmer, but not an ordinary, peasant farmer. Elisha had twelve yoke of oxen to plough his farm. In those days, using oxen to plough is like using tractors on the farm these days. In those days, Elisha had twelve oxen for ploughing. He was a mechanized farmer, a big time rich farmer. He had twelve tractors, all in his farm. He was not farming or working with cutlasses and hoes, he farmed with modern equipment of the day. Besides this, Elisha was an experienced farmer. He knew how to drive oxen for ploughing the farm. He had also people working on his farm, at least eleven servants driving eleven oxen, while he drove the twelfth.

In the secular world, Elisha was a successful man. Now that he was called of God into the work of the ministry, the vision he had in his secular business to be the head and not the tail, he also applied in the work of the ministry. Having overcome the destroyers of destiny, he and Elijah crossed the Jordan. At the point of determining his destiny, there was a separation between Elisha and the destroyers of destiny.

"And fifty men of the sons of the prophets went, and stood to view afar off: and they two (Elijah and Elisha) stood by Jordan.

And Elijah took his mantle, and rapped it together, and smote the waters, and they were divided hither and thither, so that they two went over on dry ground.

And it came to pass when they were gone over, that Elijah said unto Elisha, ask what I shall do for thee, before I be taken away from thee" (2 Kings 2:7-9).

Put no limit

Enemies will not for ever afflict. Every problem has a date of beginning and a terminal date. Temptation is not for eternity, there is a point in time, when the tempter will leave for a while, looking for another better opportunity. At both Bethel and Jericho, the sons of

GBENGA ODUNIYI

the prophets had come to trouble Elisha, to discourage and frustrate him. When Elijah and Elisha got to Jordan, fifty sons of the prophets still stood afar off to mock Elisha, however here, the Lord brought a separation between Elisha and the destroyers of destiny. In other words, when the time came for Elisha to speak out his vision, God brought a separation between Elisha and his foes. Earlier in the days of Moses, the Lord had said this to the Israelites in the wilderness.

"Say unto them, As truly as I live, saith the Lord, as ye have spoken in my ears, so will I do to you" (Numbers14:28).

When Elisha heard his master asking him of what he wanted, Elisha knew that was a time to speak his vision. In the secular world he was great, now he has to determine what his life would be like as a prophet of God.

All that the Lord wanted from Elisha at this point was to speak the word, nothing else. Do you know that Jesus has given us the same opportunity to shape, mould and determine our destiny? Jesus gave us the same opportunity when He was speaking to His disciples in John 14:14 saying;

"If ye shall ask anything in my name, I will do it".

This word of the Lord shows clearly that our destiny is in our hands. Yes, God created both the rich and the poor. However, you need to know that He is not responsible for the poverty in the life of the poor. If the poor would care to know and do what is required of him to move out of poverty, he will cease to be poor. When the sick will seek to know and do what God has laid down for his healing and deliverance, he will surely enjoy good health.

When the Lord said, if we shall ask anything in His name, He will do it, I believe the Lord knew what He was saying, even as He has declared that none of His word will go unfulfilled. As a believer, I chose to believe every word that comes out of the mouth of the Lord. Honestly, I take the word "anything" in that scriptural verse to mean anything. And the word "anything" actually means all things! Whatever you need in life to enjoy abundant life is included in that "anything".

When I came to Austria in 2001 leaving my family in Nigeria, I

90

discovered that under normal circumstances, by my status then, it could take close to ten years before my family could join me. However, I have learnt that as a child of God I am not under any circumstance. Because the word of God says he that comes from above is above all. Not only that, I strongly believe that my success and progress can't be limited by any human laws and customs. Because the Bible says that the Most High rules in the kingdom of men. In the year 2002 when I came to the knowledge of "*If ye shall ask anything in my name, I will do it*", I went to the Lord in prayer. At the end of that year I listed my prayer requests. Friend, for man, those things were impossible requests, but certainly not with God. Among the list was that I wanted to have my family to join me by 2003. Yes, they did not join me that year. However, by December 2003 God gave me a miracle job that changed my status, and later afforded me opportunity to invite my wife and my children to come and live permanently with me. By July 2004, they joined me. Many people that knew me wondered how it happened. But I know how it happened. He told me to ask for anything, and I understood having my family to join me here was part of "*If ye shall ask anything in my name, I will do it*".

I want to challenge you not to limit God's blessing in your life, for He has not put any limit to the level of His blessing and anointing He wants to release upon your life, that is why He said it many times that you should ask and that you shall receive. The man Elisha knew this and that shows in the amount of anointing he asked for. Now, your knowledge of the size and amount of the resources a man has will determine what you will ask him. If you were told that the person standing before you worth 50,000 US Dollars, and that you are allowed to ask from him anything you want. I am sure that you will not ask him for a million US Dollars. Now, if another person is brought before you and you were told that he is the richest man in the whole world, and that he has chains of companies in every nation of the world. Then they told you to ask him for anything, and such request will be granted. Of course you know that it will be foolish to ask him for one million US Dollars, even though this is a big amount.

How much more the Lord God, the Possessor of heaven and the earth?

"And Elisha said, I pray thee, let a double portion of thy spirit be upon me" (2 Kings 2:9).

Elisha knew that Elijah was a great prophet. There had never been a powerful prophet like Elijah in Israel after his death. He was so great that he could not be arrested by the soldiers of any nation. He could through the Spirit of the Lord make the word of God cease to operate in the land of Israel for three years and six months. In the days of Noah for instance, God had promised;

"While the earth remaineth seedtime and harvest, and cold and heat, and summer and winter, and day and night shall not cease" (Genesis 8:22).

However, by the word of Elijah, seedtime and harvest, as well as cold ceased. In the land of Israel, there was no dew, no rain for three and a half years. The breeze cools the day, the dew cools the night, but for that period, there was neither rain nor dew. Elijah was a mighty prophet. A vision-less man would be satisfied to be like Elijah. But for Elisha, it would be foolish to ask for the same portion of the spirit of Elijah. He knew that if he had the same portion of the spirit of Elijah, then, he would not be able to exceed what Elijah had done. He also knew that if you do not do more than your master, you will be quickly and easily forgotten in history. The successor is expected to be better than the predecessor that he may bring renewal to the work of the ministry. For what God has prepared for every one of us, eyes have not seen it, ears have not heard it and they are things that have not entered into the hearts of men. Every one of us has unique contributions to make as we receive the batons to run the race set before us. The Lord also knows this truth therefore He has put us in the same position Elisha found himself. Read this word of Jesus.

"Verily, verily, I say unto you, He that believeth on me, the works that I do shall he do also; and greater works than these shall he do; because I go unto my Father" (John 14:12).

Jesus has ordained all of us that believe in Him to do greater works, miracles, signs and wonders than He did. The Lord knew that if we do less than or the same works that He did, then, there shall be no progress in evangelism. If the greatest number of people that attended the crusade of Jesus was twenty thousand souls, then, there is hindrance to the spread of the gospel if we are unable to minister to greater number of people. The Lord knew that the gospel can only spread throughout the world if only we do greater works than His.

Elisha had a vision. His vision was not to be a duplicate, a replica, a second class man in the ministry. Elijah was like a prophet without an equal. Elisha too wanted to be unique. An athlete that breaks no record to set another has little or no fame in athletics. For your name to be written in gold, you must achieve what others have never achieved. It is no humility to refuse to be greater than your pastor. Rather, it is an ignorance being used by the devil to destroy the destiny of man. It is no humility but stupidity to believe that God will make you to achieve as much as He wants you to achieve. The Lord has given us a blank cheque; it is left for us to write on it what we desire. Moses demanded to see the glory of God, he saw the glory passing. He saw the glory of God from the beginning of creation up till the day he prayed to see the glory.

Consider the First book of Chronicles, it was not written as an interesting book to read, rather, it was written to put the record straight. The early part of the book seems boring to many people simply because only names and figures were written. However, whenever the chronicler—the writer of the book got to some people who had "greater worth", people of no less importance in the sight of God—the chronicler would pause and mention the important things in their lives. As he was writing the history for the Israelites in the captivity, he got to Jabez, and then he paused to mention the spectacular thing about Jabez. When he made mention of the brave warriors that left Saul to join David, as he got to the men of Issachar, he added one thing that differentiated them from other brave warriors; *"Men of Issachar, who understood times and knew what Israel should do..."* 1 Chronicles 12:32 (NIV). At a time, the chronicler was mentioning the number of children of the singers appointed to minister at the temple, when he got to Heman, he did not want us to just know that Heman had many children, no. He made a statement that distinguished Heman from other people who only had many children just for the sake of it. He wrote this concerning Heman "They were given him through the promises of God to exalt him. God gave Heman fourteen sons and three daughters" (I Chronicles 25:5). Unless there is something that differentiates you from others, you may be lost in the crowd. Covetousness is a sin. However, there are some great things you can covet without you being seen as a sinner by God.

"*But covet earnestly the best gifts*" (I Corinthians 12:31).

What you can covet seriously without being a sinner are not ordinary spiritual gifts rather the best gifts. Yes, the best gifts! Elisha-the man of vision knew this, he asked for the double portion of Elijah's spirit. As he prospered in his secular business, so also he saw himself prospering and flourishing in the work of the ministry. He wanted to be the head and not the tail in all spiritual matters.

A Man of Vision Nurses No fear

Many who would have made it in life, that would have done great harms against the kingdom of darkness through evangelism and the demonstration of the power of the Holy Spirit have failed because, when they first had the vision in their heart, they entertained fear. The fear of what people would say; what the reaction of people would be; "Perhaps they will think I am going too far".

A true man of vision is never afraid of what people will say, what the reactions of people might be. Ordinarily, we would have thought that Elijah would rebuke Elisha on hearing his request. Perhaps Elijah would say; "*Hey! You mean you want to be greater than me? You a farmer, aren't you grateful that I called you in the first place to give you the opportunity to replace me? What a greedy man you are!*" Fear such as these are fired into our heart by the destroyers of destiny, that we may not take the giant step in life to achieve greater things. If your vision or what you are doing is biblical, go ahead and fear no fear, for our God is the Fear to all fears and the Fear of all fears.

Some other fear that often comes to our heart is where to get the money to finance the programme or the project of our vision. Due to this fear, many children of God have settled for less, they abandon great capital intensive evangelical projects that would have had great impact on souls winning while they settle for the less effective projects. This same fear has succeeded in crippling the destiny of many people. They envisioned great business project, highly capital intensive, still highly profitable. However, here is the man without any money. Rather than abandoning the idea on the basis that there is no money to execute it, I think there is a better option. You can thank God for the idea and thereafter write the vision on a paper, place it before the Lord day and night while you pray it, confess the fulfilment of the vision and prophesy the success of the project to the glory of God.

I once found myself in such a position. Sometimes in the year 2003, I decided to write my wishes for the next few years. If you were opportune to see what I wrote and you also knew my status in Austria, unless you have a great faith, you would count the requests to be a way of tempting the Lord. However, I had earlier been taught by the Lord that with man these things are not possible but not with God, for with God all things are possible. Of course, what I wrote down were part of all things that are possible with God. So, I wrote the prayer requests down, but I called it vision. On top of the sheet of paper I wrote out this Scripture Habakkuk 2:3. Almost every time I remembered that I needed those things, I would bring the paper out, and say words like this; "I have written down this vision, I make it plain on this paper so that I can run with it. I indeed run with this vision as I read you in Jesus name. This vision is for an appointed time, it will speak. My vision shall not be silent, it shall speak, it shall not lie because it is true. Though it tarries, I Gbenga Oduniyi will wait for it, because the word of God says it will surely come, it will not tarry." Then, I will mention the first request and the time I have allotted to it. Of course I did not receive all of them at the time I wrote in that paper, but friends, I received those requests miraculously earlier than the time it was humanly possible. Everything fell into place. God worked it out in less than one and a half years the vision for the period was fully fulfilled. When we are sure that we are God's children and we have a vision but notice that the means to fulfil the vision is impossible, what we should do is to turn the impossibility aspect to God to handle while we deal with the possibility aspect of it. You wonder about the possibility aspect of it? It is the prayer strategy, the demonstration of faith in the ability of God. You must make the thoughts in your heart to be in alignment with your confession. In other words, if your confession is success and possibility, the thoughts going on in your mind should not be failure and impossibility.

As a man of vision you should know quite well that there are always giants waiting to scare you away at the promised-land. You must therefore learn not to be afraid since the Lord is with you. Remember the saying; one with God is a majority. Once you have the support of the Lord, with a stone you can kill Goliath, with five loaves and little fish you can feed thousands of people. Once the Lord is with you, storm shall be quiet and made still. The man of vision sees no obstacle. All that he sees is his vision and the Lord that leads him on. He knows that nothing can hinder God, then since he has God by himself, nothing will hinder him from achieving his goal. Vision-less men always see the enemies in action, they often see the devil working against them, and demons appearing too often to hinder them. The man of vision however will be surprised if enemies do not arise to hinder him. It will be abnormal if the devil leaves him alone to achieve his vision just like that. He knows that the devil can not support him to achieve his goal. Since the Lord is with him as a mighty warrior, a man of vision fears no evil.

What vision do you have for your life? Before going into marriage, even now that you are married, what vision do you have for your marriage? You have a vision, what type do you have? Many went into marriage without a vision, many with wrong vision; they have therefore been swept away by the winds of life. In your business, job and endeavour, do you have a vision? How big is your vision? Behold, if the vision for your business is small scale in nature, when the Lord opens the door for large scale business for you, out of ignorance and for the fear of unknown, you may close the door by your own hands. As a child of God do you have a vision? It is good that you have a vision to enter His kingdom. But that is not enough, what do you desire to achieve on earth to the glory of the Lord? Is your vision in life meant to satisfy your mortal flesh, a life fashioned after the order of Methuselah that lived 969 years on earth without any record of good thing he did in the presence of God, other than he was born, and he also had children, male and female, and then he died. What a wasted life! What an empty life!

The portion of the Lord's anointing upon Elijah was great. It was an anointing without equal. Yet, Elisha asked for the double portion of that anointing, for he knew that with God nothing shall be impossible. He knew that God has all things in abundant. He also knew that no matter how much you ask, you cannot deplete that stock of the Lord. What is the essence of anointing a successor that will not be greater than the predecessor in grace, deeds and works? The Lord therefore gives us opportunity to be greater than Him. If you succeed your pastor, and the congregation of the church does not increase (even when there are still unbelievers around you), if the church can not have greater result-oriented soul-winning programme, if the members of the Church do not increase in holiness and faithfulness in their service to God: then, your presence in that position is worse than having no one to replace the predecessor. Jesus gave us perfect example of what He wants us to be as successors. He said that we that will succeed Him will do more than He did.

The man that laid hand on Paul to heal him of his blindness and impact Holy Spirit on him was a not-too-known disciple of the Lord in Damascus, he was by name Ananias. Before and after Acts 9, this man's name was not mentioned. Yet, he was the one God chose to lay hands on Paul.

"And immediately there fell from his eyes as it had been scales: and he received sight forthwith, and arose, and was baptized" (Acts 9:18).

That same day, Paul was healed and received Holy Ghost baptism, for the Lord had sent Ananias for that purpose. (Acts 9:17)

The level of the anointing of the man that lay hands on you does not really determine what you will become. What determines what you become is what you have on your inside. As a Church worker or a minister of God, you need to study the Word of God. Sit down, have a vision for your tomorrow. Learn to plan for your future. Your sitting today will determine your rising tomorrow. The quality of the time you spend in your sitting will determine the level of your rising. Consider Paul the apostle, after he was called, he went to Arabia where he spent about three years to learn at the feet of Christ, he got loaded up and thereafter he began his ministry. The man that can not sit down to plan properly for his life can not rise above his contemporaries. God is not going to replace a legend with a vision-less man, hence, God is not limited in His choice and selection of a replacement by denomination, nationality or race, so that he can choose the best man for replacement.

Chapter Seven
A Vision for a Mission

Mission to fulfil vision

One thing is to have a vision. It is another thing to make that vision a mission. Many visionary Christians have died without seeing their visions fulfilled. The vision is the goal, the mission is the way to achieving the vision. Once the vision will bring fame, success, glory and prosperity, then the man of vision must be ready to fight some battles. Every vision of a child of God that brings glory and honour to the name of the Lord automatically brings shame and dishonour to the devil and all his demons. Therefore, since the vision has glory, the demons of failure and poverty will wage war against every step taken towards achieving the vision. They will arise to frustrate the man of vision. Until they finally fail, they will not stop the fight. Thank-God we have Jesus, thus we are more than conquerors!

Many claim to have a vision but do not know how to achieve it. But really, no one has a vision and lacks how to achieve it except the vision is not clear. When you receive a vision through the help of the

Holy Spirit, you receive alongside with it how to achieve it. However, for the Holy Spirit to lead you successfully, you must be a friend of the word of God. Now it is not as if when you study the word of God you will find expressly what you should do. It is not always so. But, the study of the Word makes you to be acquainted with the Author of the Word which is the Holy Spirit. Suppose you seek the face of the Lord concerning a job you want to take up. Of course the name of the company can not be found in the Bible as you study the Word, however, as you study the Word, the Holy Spirit will speak to you as He explains the Word to you, by this, you get to recognize His voice better, hence when He later instructs you on your vision, the voice will not sound strange to you. The Lord therefore told Joshua to study the word day and night so that he would have a good success. Good success is guaranteed when you are led by the Lord.

It must be noted that the vision is greater than the mission. No matter how beautiful, glorious and fruitful a mission may be, if it will not achieve the God-given vision, then the mission is a failure. In other words, no matter how great what you are doing now may be, if it will not take you to the promised-land, it is better to stop such activities. In fact, any mission that fails to achieve your vision is an activity without productivity. Just as your vision must satisfy your God-given destiny for your life, so it is with your mission, what you spend each day of your life doing. If what you spend the whole of today doing offers nothing good to help you achieve your vision, today is as good as a wasted day. The reason is that your God-given vision represents what God specifically sent you into this world to achieve. Every thought, decision and action you take must receive God's approval and support. You cannot follow your own way because you did not give yourself the vision in the first place.

"All the ways of a man are clean in his eyes; but the Lord weigheth the spirits" (Proverb 16:2).

"There is a way which seemeth right unto a man, but the end thereof are the ways of death" (Proverb 14:12).

It is therefore not good to go on a mission when you know that it will not help in achieving your vision. It is the vision that determines the mission, not vice versa. Thank-God that the man Elisha had a vision, the vision to be the head, not the tail in all that he does. Since a glorious vision is a target of the enemy, Elisha's action showed that he was well prepared and determined to achieve his vision.

God prepares you ahead...

The day that the Lord would take Elijah to heaven was not hidden. The sons of the prophets knew that day. Both Elijah and Elisha also knew that day. Eventually, when that day finally came Elijah said to Elisha;

"Tarry here, I pray thee; for the Lord hath sent me to Bethel" (2 Kings 2:2).

Prior to this day, Elisha had been with Elijah for about five years. But now, Elijah told him, stay here please as I go to Bethel. How on earth could Elisha accept that when actually there had not been impartation of power upon Elisha? Why would Elisha leave his farm to follow Elijah for about five years, only to be separated from him when the glory was very close?

"And Elisha said unto him, As the Lord liveth, and as thy soul liveth, I will not leave thee. So they went down" (2 Kings 2:2).

For three consecutive times Elijah told Elisha *"Tarry here, I pray thee"* Three times also Elisha answered *"As the Lord liveth, and as thy soul liveth, I will not leave thee."*

Why did Elijah tell Elisha to stay away when he knew that it was impossible for Elisha to go back into his former farm profession? Did Elijah hate Elisha? Why telling him to stay away when he knew that the day of glory had come? Elijah never hated Elisha, rather, what was happening was part of trials before Elisha. His faith and obedience must be tested. Before the Lord, Elisha was qualified to replace Elijah, God was pleased with him. He had a vision; he was humble and obedient to have answered the call almost immediately, as he surrendered all to God and trusted God for his tomorrow. God was satisfied with Elisha. For better understanding of this, let us consider similar thing that happened concerning the Lord. God knew His dear Son, and He was pleased with Jesus.

"And Jesus, when He was baptized, went up straightway out of the

water; and, lo, the heavens were opened unto Him, and He saw the Spirit of God descending like a dove, and lighting upon Him: And lo a voice from heaven, saying, This is my beloved son, in whom I am well pleased" (Matthew 3:16-17).

The God of heaven and the earth was pleased, but the devil—the prince of this world must have an encounter with Jesus. Jesus must prove Himself so that the devil might give Him His due respect.

Avoid manifestation of the flesh—anger

"Then was Jesus led up of the Spirit into the wilderness to be tempted of the devil" (Matthew 4:1).

It was the Holy Spirit that led Jesus to the wilderness, a place where Jesus would be tempted. Somebody said; "What! The Holy Spirit led Jesus to be tempted of the devil?" That the Holy Spirit led Jesus into the wilderness, I believe the Holy Spirit was like saying to Jesus; "Son, come on, I am with you, follow me to where the tempter is waiting for you" How could Jesus fail when the Holy Spirit was the One leading Jesus? Certainly no failure! For forty days Jesus was tempted, for the forty days also, Jesus did not manifest a slightest evil habit. The devil kept tempting Jesus one after the other; he tempted Jesus in all ways that Jesus might misbehave and thus be trapped. But Jesus remained faithful to God, He held on to the testimony God gave about Him, He would not for any reason disappoint God.

*"For we have not an high priest which cannot be touched with the feelings of our infirmities; but was **in all points** tempted like as we are, yet without sin."* Hebrews 4:15.

"For in that He Himself hath suffered being tempted, He is able to succour them that are tempted" (Hebrews 2:18).

Flee sin to make the devil flee before you

We all will be led and tested by God to check our obedience and our passion to prove that great and greater vision can be committed to us. When Jesus went through this process, none of the works of the flesh outlined in Galatians 5:19-21 could manifest in Christ Jesus. Therefore, at the end when Jesus cast out the devil, the devil had no choice but to leave. What makes us weak before the devil and demons, and makes us struggle to cast them out, is because we toy with the "little sins" forgetting that just a small leak can sink a great ship. When you flee from sin and from all appearance of evil, the devil will be too weak to resist your command. The Bible tells us to resist the devil, and many sermons have been preached on that. But little has been taught on what the Scriptures tell us to flee from. We do not flee from the devil, rather we resist him, bind him and cast him out. He is a toy in our hands to throw away, ball before our feet to kick around. But when it comes to the works of the flesh, the habits and sins the flesh takes pleasure in, the Bible says we should flee from them. The Scriptures command; flee fornication, flee idolatry, flee youthful lust. You do not play or joke with sin and temptation when your destiny is at stake. Sin destroys destiny. Anytime the devil mounts pressure on you to commit sin and it's like the pressure is too much or greater than your strength, friend, that is the time the glory is at your door step. You must flee from sin. Do not bind that adulterous woman who tries to lure you into sin. Flee from her! (Read 2 Timothy 2:22; I Timothy 6:1-11; I Corinthians 6:18 and 10:14). Few days before He went to the cross, the Lord had this testimony.

"The prince of this world cometh, and hath nothing in me" (John 14:30).

That was a man of vision. Jesus did not hold on to anything that could be associated with the devil, therefore, the devil could not exercise any control over Jesus. He would not allow anything to separate Him from His vision. When Elijah said to Elisha after they had returned from Gilgal; "Tarry here, I pray thee" He said the same at Bethel and repeated the same at Jericho. Elisha was not annoyed. He never allowed the spirit of anger to manifest in his life. He did not rebel either by calling Elijah all sort of names. Rather, Elisha would say; "As the Lord liveth, and thy soul liveth, I will not leave thee".

The Lord has no pleasure in the use of violent, rebellious, angry vessels. If the spirit of violence, the demon of rebellion and the spirit of anger dwell in you, there is no way you can be full of the Holy Spirit, for then, you will be full of part of demons and part of the Holy Spirit. No man that is full of the Holy Spirit has any room in his life for the devil. More so, it is not possible to be full of both the Holy Spirit and demons, for no servant can serve two masters at the same time. Act of rebellion made God to cast the devil out of heavens. He will not entertain a rebellious vessel.

If you are an angry man, one that easily loses his anger, you can not have your vision fulfilled. Do not rejoice that you are great now, who knows whether what you have now is like dew instead of rain of achievement that the Lord wants for your life. No matter the spiritual gifts you may have, the Scriptures can not be broken. The Lord has absolutely nothing to do with an angry man or woman.

"Make no friendship with an angry man; and with a furious man thou shall not go" (Proverbs 22:24).

Though Elisha had been faithful to the call of the Lord all along, if he had become angry with Elijah, he would have lost out. He would have missed the double anointing. If the word of God commands us not to make friendship with an angry man, then you should know that God is not a friend but an enemy of an angry man.

"...With furious man thou shall not go."

The journey of Elisha could have terminated either when they returned from Gilgal, at Bethel or at Jericho if Elisha had become furious with Elijah. But why is God telling us not to be a friend with an angry man and not to go on a mission with a furious man?

"Be not hasty in thy spirit to be angry: for anger rested in the bosom of fools" (Ecclesiastes 7:9).

"He that is soon angry dealeth foolishly" (Proverbs 14:17).

Potential legends are not hypocrites

The first spirit that leads man away from his vision is the spirit of anger. Elisha overcame that through subtle words. Besides this, in his answer to Elijah, Elisha refused and rejected hypocritical humility. He was just frank and sincere. He knew that all he wanted was the anointing, and that, to receive the anointing, he must be rightly positioned, close to Elijah. He told Elijah frankly, "I will follow you, where you go there I shall go, and nothing will separate me from you until my vision is fulfilled". A man of vision is not crafty, cunning or dubious. It does not matter if the people misunderstand you, or become annoyed. You must be truthful, sincere and faithful. A man of vision that desires to achieve his vision is a friend of the truth, and a lover of truth. Anything that opposes the truth opposes Christ Jesus, for Jesus is the truth. In your mission towards achieving your vision, girt your loins about with truth. Being truthful will make you enjoy the favour of the Lord. Be faithful in the little that is committed into your hand today, for greater things shall be committed to your hand tomorrow based on your faithfulness today.

Elisha wanted to follow Elijah, and so, he did not hide his mission from his master. He was not diplomatic about the issue; rather he was sincere and straight forward. Elisha did not bother himself with what could happen if he insisted to follow Elijah, he did not choose to do it with earthly wisdom. He damned all the consequences; he did not fear the negative effect of his sincerity of purpose. Many are anointed children of God that have derailed from the mission that actually leads to the fulfilment of their vision because of certain fear they nursed. They fear both the known and the unknown. Before they take a step, they will want to identify the likely problems and when such likely problems are identified, every step they take on their mission is guided by the fear of the effect or the implication of the identified problems. The Bible clearly tells us that fear has torment. Our God is the Fear of all fears and Fear to all fears. You do not tell God you have big problem, rather let your problem know that you have a Very Big God. It is high-time we allow our problems experience the mighty power of the Almighty God, rather than learning and practising how the people of the world do their things. The antidote to all forms of fear is the command from the Scripture that God alone should be our fear. When you attack every form of fear with the "fear of the Lord" as a weapon in your hand, the result is wonderful. It has worked for me, and I know it will work for you if you will employ this weapon that will make all fears to begin to fear your presence.

"Thus saith the Lord, Learn not the way of the heathen, and be not dismayed at the signs of heaven; for the heathen are dismayed at

them."

"Be not dismayed at their faces, lest I confound thee before them. And they shall fight against thee, but they shall not prevail against thee; for I am with thee saith the Lord, to deliver thee" (Jeremiah 10:2; 1:17&19).

The fear of likely problems has destroyed the destiny of many people. Many are pastors these days that are afraid of preaching the gospel truth. They cannot caution some very few individuals in the Church whose life-style is worse than unbelievers. Such people hold high positions in the Church, yet the pastors, whom the Bible called overseers, cannot correct or melt out discipline against such people. You want to know why? Such people are wealthy, the pastors are afraid if such rich people begin to leave the Church, how then will the Church pay all its bills? Yet, such pastors will preach at the pulpit, "My God shall supply all your needs according to His riches in glory in Christ Jesus" Thus, apart from the fact that fear has made such pastors to lack faith in God's ability to provide for the needs of the Church, such pastors are being pastured by those few powerful corrupt rich carnal people in the Church. Such pastors allowed their mission to change their glorious vision. Because such people are terrified at the sight of such problems, God terrifies them in the faces of such problems. The reason being that, the man that fears his enemy, demons, the devil or problems, is a disgrace to God in the presence of His foes. God is not friendly with people that fear in the face of tribulation. God is hindered from performing signs and wonders when man is afraid. The reason is that the position of a man that is afraid is worse than the state of an unbeliever. The moment fear comes into the heart of man, faith goes out. Fear kills destiny, therefore you must overcome fear. The will of God for His children is this;

"Sanctify the Lord of hosts Himself; and let Him be your fear, and let Him be your dread" (Isaiah 8:13).

If there is anything that we must fear, it must be the Lord of hosts. Should we be dreadful of anything, it must be the Lord of hosts. If however you fear someone or something else, it means you are not afraid of God, you count the Lord God Almighty insignificant while you recognise, respect and fear things and people that are below in might and created by God. It is a great insult to God. To make your vision your mission therefore, means to fear no other person or other thing other than God. Let the problems manifest, let the people react and over-react, if God be for you, He will deal with them all, you will leave the stage with a smile on your face. Only fear the Lord alone. The fear of what Elijah would say for insisting on following him three times did not make Elisha to become hypocritical. If you want to move from the class of babes to the class of legends, it is important that you avoid hypocrisy.

Be quick to identify and avoid distractions

"And the sons of the prophets that were at Bethel came forth to Elisha, and said unto him, Knowest thou that the Lord will take away thy master from thy head to day? And he said, Yea, I know it; hold ye your peace" (2 Kings 2:3).

During a mission to a vision there are distractions on the way, aimed at slowing down the speed of man, to make him stray out of the right path and/or to frustrate him, to make him a failure. Anybody can be used. Of course the devil is not foolish to have used someone you have little or no regard for. When the devil wanted to place stumbling block in the way of Christ to the cross, he spoke through the apostle that had just impressed the Lord, the man that had just received a wonderful revelation from God of who Jesus was. The devil spoke through Peter against the vision and the destiny for which purpose Christ came into this world. But Jesus did not waste time to rebuke Satan that spoke through Peter.

"But He turned, and said unto Peter, Get thee behind me, Satan: thou art an offence unto me" (Matthew 16:23).

Likewise for Elisha, he did not encourage conversation with the sons of the prophets, he told them, "Yes I know but you shut up!" That was the word. The man that will fulfil destiny, that will see his vision come true must be able to discern every spirit that converse with him. He must remain focused, he can not have discussions with every one on earth, he must be reserved yet not pompous. The right mission of Elisha at that time was to be with his master, not to allow anything to serve as means of separation. But the issue raised by the sons of the prophets was an interesting one. If well discussed, the Spirit of the Lord might give them more details about the departure of Elijah. The discussions could as well help them to arrange a befitting programme whereby they would tap some anointing from Elijah, at least they might tell him to lay his hands on them all as Moses did in the wilderness for the seventy leaders of the people. But really, all that was out of the vision of Elisha, his vision then was personal not corporate, collective or general. For there is time for everything on earth. An attempt to plant during harvest time and hoping to reap during planting season is a great design for complete failure and shame. There is the time to attend to personal needs, and there is the time to focus on the needs of others. Hence we are made to God as priests and kings. As priests we attend to ourselves on our knees before the Father. As kings we rise on our feet to use our authority and issue commands before the hosts of heaven, earth and hell, and all of them are made to be obedient to us. He that will make his vision his mission does not mix up issues.

Never assume that distractions and hindrances will come only once, you must persevere because they will continue to come until your vision is fully fulfilled. Do you have a vision to make heaven? Then know for sure that distractions and temptation will continue to come until you depart from this world. Whatever vision you have for the ministry committed to your hand by the Lord, even for your marriage, for your children, until you achieve that vision, distractions will not stop to come. But as the vision is fulfilled, shame and disgrace will make the devil to disappear before you. Consider the case of Job, the devil came before the Lord in chapter One and later in chapter Two, but when he discovered that Job would not give up until he achieved his vision, from Chapter three to Chapter forty-two, the devil was ashamed to appear before the Lord on the case of Job. I know that even if God would call Satan and asked him of the case of Job, Satan would tell the Lord, "Let's forget him, Lord". Thus, making your vision your mission means being determined to fulfil destiny, readiness not to settle for anything less than the vision. It means that you will have unfailing faith as long as there is breath in you, the vision will be fulfilled. You must come to a point where you believe that not even death is able to separate you from your vision. It entails endurance and perseverance.

Go for God's maximum

"And it came to pass, when they were gone over, that Elijah said to Elisha, Ask what I shall do for thee, before I be taken away from thee" (2 Kings 2:9).

This was the glorious moment Elisha had been waiting for. To say with his own mouth what his destiny would be. For some people, there is nothing more now, they can begin to relax, for they have reached their goals in life. To them, everything is settled, nothing can alter their destiny. But that was not it. Elisha had just reached the last hurdle but the most difficult of all.

"And Elisha said, I pray thee, let a double portion of your spirit be upon me.

And he said, thou hast asked a hard thing: nevertheless, if thou see me when I am taken from thee, it shall be so unto thee; but if not, it shall not be so" (2 Kings 2:9-10).

The call upon Elisha was to replace Elijah, however, concerning how mighty in anointing he would be, it was left in the hand of Elisha to determine. Thus he was given a blank cheque. Not even Elijah was in a good position to determine the destiny of Elisha, no, God did not leave the destiny of a replacement completely in the hand of the predecessor. The successor has to determine that by himself. Of course you will notice from the answer of Elijah that if he were to ask for Elisha, though he was a great and powerful man of God, still, somehow, for one reason or the other Elijah would not go to the extent of asking for double portion for Elisha, for that was a big and difficult thing. Ordinarily without any harm Elijah would not consider double portion anointing necessary. But Elisha did not want to be ordinary, therefore, he did not ask for ordinary anointing. He would not want to be simple in anointing, therefore he asked for difficult anointing. This to Elijah was difficult because it was beyond what any man can grant. Now you can imagine the gravity of the request of Elisha when someone like Elijah said, "Thou hast asked a hard thing..." That was Elijah. In fact, I am sure, not even Elijah would have asked for such anointing for himself. But the truth is that, Elijah was never in the shoe of Elisha, therefore, Elijah couldn't have thought as Elisha would think. The truth is that you are the only person that knows how much you can ask for, because only you also know how much you lack. The Bible says, with God, everything is possible. Elisha did not want an anointing granted by man but the one granted by God the owner and giver of anointing. If the Lord chooses you to take over from your pastor, the level of the anointing you will get greatly depends on your desire, your goal, and your vision. For if the Lord would decide to give you more than you desire, your lack of desire would make the anointing idle and worthless. When a brilliant student has no interest in passing out of the institution with First Class, though he has all it takes to get it, but for his lack of interest, he would finish with a class lower than First Class. It is easy to fail than to be successful.

To determine the level of His anointing upon your life, God leaves you to decide that. But no matter how much you ask, your demand can not exceed or deplete the stock of the Lord.

"And so shall the knowledge of wisdom be unto thy soul: when thou hast found it, then there shall be a reward, and thy expectation shall not be cut off" (Proverbs 24:14).

As Christians, God's chosen generation and as potential legends we must learn to allow the size of God's limitless resources to determine the magnitude of our request. God is a loving Father; He wants us to have our own expectations, anticipations. God willingly allows us to fix our desires because He knows the resources at His disposal, He knows that no matter how much we may ask, He is abundantly able to meet our needs and even do more than we may ask or think. There is surely an end to every mission, to every event. The word of God gives us this assurance that our expectation will not be cut off. If you think big and expect big, your expectation shall not be cut off. Similarly, if you think little and expect little, that expectation shall not be cut off. Even if the thought is big but the expectation is little, the word of God says it is the expectation that shall not be cut off. It does not matter what the expectation is, positive or negative, big or small, there is the assurance for us; our expectation shall not be cut off. Hence we should be positive in our thinking. Not only that, we should think of good things and not evil.

Elijah was kind and generous, he wanted to bless Elisha, anything Elisha would ask shall be granted, but he under-estimated Elisha, for Elisha's request was beyond Elijah's expectation. Elisha's request was simply beyond what Elijah believed he as a person could grant. Elisha however did not ask for Elijah's maximum, rather, he asked for God's maximum. However, this request placed before him another hurdle to cross. The request of Elisha was a difficult thing to be granted by Elijah, therefore Elijah said;

"And he said, Thou hast asked a hard thing: nevertheless, if thou see me when I am taken from thee, it shall be so unto you; but if not, it shall not be so" (2 Kings 2:10).

Be eager to take up responsibility

The request of Elisha was beyond Elijah's ability and resources. That great expectation therefore brought another hurdle between Elisha and his vision. Now, he had to be watchful, vigilant to see Elijah when he would be taken away if his vision would be fulfilled.

The word of Elijah indeed put Elisha in tight corner, for there was a probability that Elisha get his desire or lose out completely. Or what do you think would happen if Elisha did not see Elijah when he was being taken away? It means Elisha would receive absolutely nothing, not even single anointing. It means he would remain the same! A lazy man that is ready to take up anything available would say; *"If the desirable is not available, the available becomes desirable"* Many people could have blamed Elisha, saying; *"He was too ambitious, an extremist!"* A man that fears a lot would have regretted asking for God's maximum. Also a lazy Christian that found himself in the position of Elisha would have got fed up with God, thinking that the Lord is demanding too much from him. But that was not the case with Elisha, he was rugged, as the Lord's liveth, he believed that his vision was attainable. He was not afraid of challenges. He was ever ready to take up responsibility if that is what it would take for him to have his vision fulfilled. He that is afraid of taking up responsibility will (soon without knowing) stray away from the mission to the fulfilment of his vision. There is no anointing without attached responsibility. No man that runs away from responsibility can be a general in the army of the Lord. Be eager to take up responsibility. As the Lord lives, you shall fulfil destiny, for your expectation shall not be cut off. For the assignment before you now, the Holy Spirit may lead you to go on a long days of continuous fasting for the glory that will follow. Do not avoid that responsibility, for an attempt to avoid that responsibility is an avenue to divert the glory that should follow. The manifestation of the so called obstacles and distractions on your mission to fulfilling your destiny simply means that you have a glorious destiny and that the destiny is real and achievable.

No matter what, the vision is possible

*"And it came to pass, as they still **went on**, and **talked**, that, behold, there appeared a chariot of fire, and horses of fire, and parted them both asunder; and Elijah went up by a whirlwind into heaven"* (2 Kings 2:11).

As Elisha and Elijah went on, they were talking, discussing some issues of interest. But Elisha did not allow that discussions to lead him away from his vision. Though he too was contributing to those discussions, he was not carried away. As they were talking, Elisha kept reminding himself of the condition given for the receipt of the double portion anointing.

"If thou see me when I am taken from thee"

Therefore, as they were talking, Elisha kept looking at Elijah. He fixed his eyes and heart on Elijah. What they were saying was less important. In fact, to him it was just to wipe away time. Before long, Elijah went up by a whirlwind to heaven.

"And Elisha saw it" (2 Kings 2:12).

That Elijah might know that he Elisha saw him, Elisha cried aloud;

"My father, my father, the chariot of Israel, and the horsemen thereof" (2 Kings 2:12).

Do not be discouraged from the pursuit of your vision, for your expectation shall not be cut off. A man of vision is rugged. He does not care what people may say. In fact, the word of faith spoken by a believer sounds in the hearing of an unbeliever as the word of pride. Have a vision for your life. Pray for a glorious vision for the ministry committed to your hand. Never go into marriage without a vision. Even if you are in marriage without any vision, do not go ahead without vision. Sit down at the feet of the Lord, conceive a vision. Make your vision your mission. A man of vision is not a friend of sins and iniquities. Rather, he separates himself from the world and holds on to his vision. Even when he is losing so many things—parents, friends, money, position and opportunities as a result of keeping to his mission for the vision, he still does not care. What matters most to him is the fulfilment of his vision, when the vision is fulfilled, he receives lasting joy. People that have once forsaken him will see the glory of the Lord upon him and will return to him. But now, as they return, they return with their faces bowed to the ground and worship God with him. When Elisha returned in the power of the double anointing, something great happened concerning the sons of the prophets who once played the role of destroyers of Elisha's destiny.

"And when the sons of the prophets which were to view at Jericho saw him (Elisha), they said, The spirit of Elijah doth rest on Elisha. And they came to meet him, and bowed themselves to the ground before him" (2 Kings 2:15).

Chapter Eight
Readiness to surrender all

"And it came to pass, that as they went in the way, a certain man said unto Him, Lord, I will follow you whithersoever thou goest" (Luke 9:57).

The Lord Jesus came to draw men to God, to show them the way to the kingdom of God, to guide and lead them on the way. When a man repents of his sinful ways and follows the Lord, there is a great joy in heaven among the angels of God. Therefore, it is expected that the Lord should rejoice when a man decides to follow Him, to worship and serve Him. The man in the above scriptural verse (on his own) made up his mind to follow the Lord. He did not just believe in his heart, he confessed it. He told the Lord, "I will follow you where ever you go." As it is, the Lord will not entrust Himself to any man, for He knew all men. He did not need man's testimony about man, for He knew what was in a man (John 2:24-25). He therefore said to the man;

"Foxes have holes, and birds of the air have nests; but the Son of

man hath not where to lay His head" (Luke 9:58).

This man could have decided to follow this miracle-worker and bread-giver based on what he could gain from being His disciple. But Jesus told him point blank, "If by following me you think I will make you to live in a mansion, you are missing the point, for I have no mansion". Do you have great interest in becoming a great minister of God so that you can be lodged in five-star hotels whenever you are invited to minister? Jesus says; "I can not assure you of that, for there were times that I had no place to sleep other than in an open boat right in the sea". Have you decided to follow Jesus so that you can build magnificent mansion? Jesus says; "I have no earthly house of my own that I built".

Though He greatly desired that people would follow Him, He has no joy in disciples that are materialistic, the fair-weather disciples. If you push material wealth before the purpose of the Master for your calling you are worse than someone that has not decided to follow Him. Therefore, material wealth should not be the main purpose for following the Lord. Even if that was what brought us to the Lord, now as we grow from babes into maturity, we should change and make right our purpose. We should re-prioritize our needs. The kingdom of God first, followed by all other things. All other things must depend on our journey to the kingdom of God, and not vice versa. Hence, the Lord commanded us to seek first the kingdom of God, and then, all other things shall be added to our pursuit of the kingdom. We need not seek material wealth, for God is committed to give them to us freely once we choose to seek His kingdom and its righteousness, that is, seeking to know the right way to live, speak and act as children of God and putting into practice what you have learnt. As you do this, God will bless you by making what the people of this world run after in other to possess, to begin to run after you.

"And He said to another, Follow me. But he said, Lord, suffer me first to go and bury my father:"

The man that first came was materialistic. Jesus thereafter called another man, but this one has great respect for culture and the society norms. He said to the Lord, "My father is dead, let me go and bury him". A school of thought conversant with the Hebrew's culture believes that the statement of the man may not necessarily mean that his father was dead, but could mean, "Give me a time, after the death of my father, I will start following you"

The man did not want to offend his parents, more especially his father. Possibly, his father was one of the antagonists of Jesus, if he now follows Jesus that might set him against his father. Hence, he would want to wait till his father kicks the bucket before he would decide on where he would spend eternity. On the other hand, if his father was indeed dead, then he wanted to do what the society expects from every child. Whether the norms of the society stand against the commandment of the Lord or not, all he would do was to plead with the Lord, "O Lord, do not be annoyed, just allow me to do this, then I will follow you".

Although the purpose of the Lord is to draw all men to God, He has no joy in the people that will rather please the society and their parents at the expense of being obedient to God.

"Jesus said unto Him, Let the dead bury their dead: but go thou and preach the kingdom of God" (Luke 9:60).

Let the society carry out its own norms, let your father practice his own belief, but you that have a great privilege of being called by the Lord, go and preach the gospel of God. The Lord is no lover of people that postpone the date of their salvation until something else happens; rather, He wants everything to depend on your salvation, not vice versa. Many people who before marriage are flirt plan to quit sexual immorality after marriage. Some other people plan to start paying their full tithe when they begin to earn good salary, but now that their salary is insufficient; they eat their fruit with the seed. They do not know that any decision that is needed to be taken today must not be postponed till tomorrow, because tomorrow will come with its own challenges on which you must take a stance.

"And another also said, Lord I will follow thee; but let me first go bid them farewell, which are at home at my house" (Luke 9:61).

This third man said to the Lord, "I will follow you, however let me go back home to say goodbye to all my people". The man wanted to announce his decision to follow the Lord to everyone even before following the Lord. He has decided to follow Jesus, but before putting his faith into practice, he wanted to announce to his world. Many people have through these means aborted the plan of God for their lives which was aimed at launching them into their healing, prosperity and breakthrough. Many drunkards before practising Christianity went to their friends at the club telling them they no more drink because they have met Jesus. Unfortunately, before they left the club, they resume drinking. Some Christians after asking the Lord's favour concerning their finances, in answer to their requests, the Lord gave them business ideas. As these ideas become too real in their heart, they expose them to people around them before the right time, thus, many died in poverty with their ideas in them. A seed sown in the soil must not be exposed if it must become fruitful.

"A fool uttereth all his mind: but a wise man keepeth it in till afterwards" (Proverbs 29:11).

"And Jesus said unto him, No man having put his hand to the plough, and looking back, is fit for the kingdom of God" (Luke 9:62).

The response of the Lord to this last man that came to Him brings us to what Elisha said to Elijah as Elijah cast his mantle upon Elisha. As Elijah was about to retire, the Lord gave him this instruction.

"Elisha the son of Shaphat of Abelmeholah shalt thou anoint to be prophet in thy room

So Elijah departed thence, and found Elisha the son of Shaphat, who was plowing with twelve yoke of oxen before him, and he with the twelft: and Elijah passed by him, and cast his mantle upon him.

And he (Elisha) left the oxen, and ran after Elijah, and said, Let me I pray thee, kiss my father and my mother, and then I will follow thee. And he (Elijah) said unto him, Go back again: for what have I done to thee?" (I Kings 19:16-20).

The word of Elisha was similar to that of the last man that spoke with Jesus in Luke 9:61, the man said, "Let me go back home to bid them farewell". And here, Elisha said to Elijah, "Let me go and kiss my father and my mother". Elijah did not rebuke Elisha for saying that, but Jesus rebuked that man. If our God is not partial, then there must be something in the request of Elisha in meaning and application which made it clearly different from the request made by that man.

"And he (Elisha) returned back from him (Elijah), and took a yoke of oxen, and slew them, and boiled their flesh with the instruments of the oxen, and gave unto the people, and they did eat. Then he arose, and went after Elijah, and ministered unto him" (I Kings 19:21).

When Elisha asked for permission to go back home to kiss his mother and his father, Elisha essentially meant to say a final goodbye to his hitherto profession. Elisha was until then a full time, large-scale, mechanized farmer. When he left Elijah, he left him to cripple his farming business. He slew the oxen and then he gathered the ploughing equipment, burnt them to cook the meat. As he slaughtered the animals, he burnt the wooden equipment used in ploughing. Invariably, he crippled his farm business. This was a man that was zealous for God and was ready to forgo all riches for the faith. In another words, what Elisha did was that he made a clean break from his past and embrace the future. We hold too much on our past, which shouldn't be.

Elisha celebrated his calling by organising a feast. Perhaps, he had been praying, coveting to be a prophet, but he was not born into the family of prophets. He was a wealthy farmer, yet he would gladly forgo everything he had for the high calling from God. The celebration of the calling was not just to feast with the people but to make his farming impossible to go back into.

He was called into the service of God without the promise of food by Elijah, yet he threw away his farm. He knew that there were days of famine, he also knew that hunger can push man to do what normally he hates to do.

"The full soul loathed an honey-comb; but to the hungry soul every bitter thing is sweet" (Proverbs 27:7).

When you have enough food and comfort, then you develop taste and become selective. But for a man that lacks food, even a spoilt food will be considered by him as not been a poison. Elisha did not want to create opportunity for him to return into farming in his life.

Immediately he left Elijah, he disconnected himself from his farm profession and then, he followed Elijah. The Bible never told us that he kissed his father and mother. Perhaps, his job was everything to him, his farm work was so dear to him, yet he abandoned it. He put it in a condition that would be impossible for him to return to.

As Elisha slew those animals, the people around could have thought he was mad. Many of them would call Elisha a religious fanatic. Some would say "Hey man, you are going too far, what if prophet-hood work is not enough to supply your needs, with what will you support yourself and the ministry?" Many people ridiculed and mocked Elisha saying; "He is new into prophet-hood, he will soon relax". They could have warned him that extreme was dangerous, but Elisha would not listen to them. He roasted the meat and gave them to eat. Elisha could have said; "Friends, you just eat and that will be enough." Remember that Elisha was not a man that encouraged conversation with the destroyers of destiny.

Elisha deliberately lost all he had worked for, just for the sake of God's work. He was ready to become poor if by working for God would mean being poor.

A young rich man once came to Jesus. He had been keeping the commandments of God ever since he was a boy.

"Then Jesus beholding him loved him, and said unto him, One thing thou lackest: go thy way, sell whatsoever thou hast, and give to the poor, and thou shall have treasure in heaven: and come, take up the cross, and follow me.

And he was sad at that saying, and went away grieved: for he had great possessions" (Mark 10:21-22).

The rich young man on hearing the word of Jesus became sad and went away grieved, because he had great wealth. He loved to follow Jesus, but he was not ready to lose all his wealth as a condition to following Jesus. There are so many people like this young man in the Church these days, they want to serve God, but not with their money. The moments they hear the Pastor speak on tithe and offering, such people become uncomfortable. Many claim to believe Jesus, but would not go to Church because they do not want to give out their money. Yes, they have many 'genuine reasons' just like this young rich man in the Scripture we read. The moment the man heard the instruction of Jesus, he became sad and grieve. But, really, Jesus was not teaching him an impossible thing; for it was a thing Jesus Himself had done and was still doing. When He wanted to come into this planet earth, He emptied Himself of His glory, and when He came into the world, He did it again.

"For ye know the grace of our Lord Jesus Christ, that, though He was rich, yet for your sakes He became poor, that ye through His poverty might be rich" (2 Corinthians 8:9).

Jesus became poor that we might be rich. He transferred His riches to us. Hence we have no reason to be poor, for Jesus was poor that we might be rich. He transferred us into riches, while He took our position of poverty. The same thing Jesus told the rich young man, sell your possession and give to the poor. But the man was not ready for that great sacrifice. The man loved pleasure of wealth. He never wanted to taste poverty, not for the sake of the gospel. The moment he heard the word of Jesus, he went away, thus he turned his back to Jesus the Saviour, even to God's kingdom. Invariably too, Jesus turned His back to the young rich man that had just gone away, while Jesus faced His disciples. What Elisha did without being forced or counselled, the young rich man refused even when it was Jesus Christ that gave him the instruction.

There was another man from the Bible that left all for the sake of the gospel, and he never had regret. The Lord Jesus was at the sea side, and the crowd was coming and becoming too large. As God had arranged it, there were two ships left there by the fishermen, who were washing their nets. Jesus entered into one of the ships and asked Peter to put out a little from shore. The Lord preached to the crowd, after the crusade he wanted to bless Peter for being kind to have given his ship for the work of the gospel. Therefore, He told Peter to put out into the deep water and let down the nets for a catch. Peter and his colleagues had toiled all night in the deep without a catch. But in obedience to the word of the Lord, he launched into the deep and let down his net.

"And when they had this done, they inclosed a great multitude of fishes: and their net brake.

And they beckoned unto their partners which were in the other ship, that they should come and help them. And they came and filled both the ships, so that they began to sink" (Luke 5:6.-7).

As Peter obeyed the Lord, he had a great catch, his net began to break, a sort of overflowing blessings, such that there shall not be enough room to receive it (Malachi 3:10). The fishes were enough to fill the two ships even then, the catch made the ships to sink. What a heavy catch they made! A net breaking, boat sinking blessing, yet nothing was missing, nothing lost. Peter, John and James were astonished, because for hours during the night when it was more ideal to catch fishes they had none. Now, for just few minutes, they had a heavy large catch, for this, Peter worshipped the Lord. Then, Jesus spoke to them saying;

"Fear not, from henceforth thou shalt catch men" (Luke 5:10).

Jesus gave them invitation to join Him in the work of the gospel. He called them to be His disciples.

"And when they had brought their ships to land, they forsook all, and followed Him" (Luke 5:11).

What would happen to the great large fish they left? Was it not their reward for being generous to the Lord? Somebody said; "Hey, you should have sold the fish and use the money to support yourselves and the gospel" But Peter, John and James left them all. They turned their eyes away from material wealth while they looked at Jesus.

Now, why would these three disciples not be preferred to the other disciples by Jesus? Peter, John and James belonged to the inner caucus of Jesus. The Lord showed them great things He never showed others. Only these three were with Him on the mountain of transfiguration. They witnessed the divine meeting on earth which Jesus had with Moses and Elijah. They listened to their discussions; they heard Jesus as He welcomed both Moses and Elijah to the meeting mentioning their names. These men watched live the discussions these two greatest prophets had with the Lord. What a great grace to hear Moses speak, and hear Elijah saying his own opinion on the greatest event that ever took place on this planet earth, the death of Jesus on the cross. They so much loved the meeting such that Peter never wanted them to leave the mount.

At another time when Jesus wanted to raise the dead daughter of Jairus back to life, all the disciples of Jesus were with Him all the way to the house of Jairus. But when it was time to demonstrate His power, the Bible has this to say;

"And He (Jesus) suffered no man to follow Him, save Peter, and James, and John the brother of James" (Mark 5:37).

Jesus went into the room where the dead girl was laid with both the father and the mother of the girl, and these three disciples. He went in with the parents that they might know what He did to their dead girl. He took in Peter, John and James that they might witness and learn the demonstration of power. The Lord loves people that are ready to surrender all for the sake of the kingdom of God. Are you ready to go hungry because of the gospel? Can you accept to be home-less, childless or poor for the sake of the gospel? Can you stake your life for the sake of the kingdom of God? We have heard of many University dons called by the Lord to preach the gospel. Some of them went as far as setting ablaze their certificates. They lost all for the sake of the gospel.

Apostle Peter once told the Lord; *"Now we have left all, and have followed you, what shall be our reward?"*

And Jesus answered and said, Verily I say unto you. There is no man that hath left house, or mother, or wife, or children, or lands, for my sake, and the gospels,

But he shall receive an hundredfold now in this time, houses, and brethren, and sisters, and mothers, and children, and lands, with persecutions; and in the world to come eternal life (Mark 10:29-30).

Study the above scriptural verse very well, whatever you give for the sake of the Lord and for the sake of the gospel, shall be repaid to you on this planet earth. You do not need mothers in heaven, for there shall not be sisters in heaven because there, there shall be no marriage for we shall all be the same. The Lord therefore said,

"But he shall receive an hundredfold now in this time" (Mark 10:30).

That which you give shall be given back to you in hundredfold. This is an assurance of prosperity and abundance for people that will give their material wealth for the sake of the Lord and for the gospel's sake. Please get this issue clear here. We are not saying that going into full-time ministry is the only way to surrender all to the Lord. Neither are we saying that selling all that you have and giving the proceeds to fund evangelism is the only way to surrender all. The truth is, as children of God, we are commanded to love the Lord God with all our heart, our soul and our mind. When you truly love the Lord, it will not be too difficult for you to give to the Lord what He requests from you. You will not find it difficult to squeeze out time out of your busy schedule in other to spend quality time with the Lord in prayer and in the study of His word, that is, if you truly love Him. If truly you have received Him as the Lord of your soul, nothing will make you to tell Him consistently "No, Lord…" without changing your mind in any aspect of your life when He instructs you to do something. Sometimes we consider what we are about to lose when we want to obey Him, for there is a price paid for every act of obedience. There is always something you have to give up as you say, "Yes, Lord" to His commandment. For instance, if the Spirit wakes you up at the middle of the night to pray, when you obey, the sleep you forgo and the "inconveniency" are the price paid. Sometimes when the Spirit leads you to give certain uncommon special offering, the price paid is inability to purchase certain things you would have bought if you have not given out the money. Perhaps, what you need to surrender could be your friendship with ungodly friends or unholy television shows. Are you ready to surrender all? If you will rise to the status of a legend, you have to set your priority. When I was in the University, I discovered that medical students rarely participate in most campus politics and shows unlike Arts students. Those who could not set their priorities right never made it beyond first or second year, as they were dropped from medicine to other departments or faculties their life-style on campus fits into. If you want to be a legend you must like Abraham let God be your reward, and like the Levites let God be your inheritance, because if God is your reward and inheritance, then you have at your disposal all that God has.

One thing is clear about God. He will not owe man anything. Nobody will give Him with a sincere heart and yet have regret. Elisha had no regret, in terms of the anointing he flourished. Still, he did not lack material wealth. The sons of the prophets who had all along been mocking and discouraging him noticed the blessings of the Lord upon his life.

"And Elisha came to Gilgal: and there was a dearth (that is, famine) in the land; and the sons of the prophets were sitting before him: and said unto his servant, set on the great pot, and seethe pottage for the sons of the prophets" (2 Kings 4:38).

In the days of famine, Elisha could still instruct his servant to set on the great pot to prepare food for his guests. He was not managing food, when people were managing the little they had, he was directing his resources to be prepared in large quantity. People that readily surrender all for the sake of the Lord and the gospel's never lack anything good, to them there are sure promises of God. Even when great multitudes are in want, they are in abundance.

"They shall not be ashamed in the evil time: and in the days of famine they shall be satisfied" (Psalm 37:19).

The sons of the prophets began to meet with Elisha in his house. They ate free food, enough food. Even when they ate poison, it could not hurt them. With little loaves of bread, Elisha fed one hundred people. Then, the sons of the prophets decided to live with Elisha permanently.

"And the sons of the prophets said unto Elisha, Behold now, the place where we dwell with thee is too strait for us.

Let us go, we pray thee, unto Jordan, and take thence every man a beam, and let us make us a place there, where we may dwell. And he answered, Go ye" (2 Kings 6:1,2).

The sons of the prophets from different places kept coming to Elisha to witness the demonstration of the power of the Lord through

124

him, to learn at his feet and to eat free food. They kept coming until the place could no longer contain them. Elisha did not regret his decision and the step that he took to give up his farming profession and possession. If you desire abundance and overflowing anointing, if you want to move from the class of babes to the class of legends, then you must be ready to surrender all. After all, what is it that you have that you did not receive? And as it is written, no one can receive unless it is given him from heaven.

Chapter Nine
Time of training

It can not be over-emphasized that Elisha hitherto had no formal training in the School of Prophet. He was a farmer. He knew little or nothing about prayer and prophecy. Elisha, at the time of his calling, had no pre-knowledge and experience concerning the ministry the Lord was about to commit into his hand.

When Elijah cast his mantle on Elisha, he could have cried; "*This can't be true. I am a farmer, I know nothing about the work of a prophet*" He could have asked so many questions; "*How will I ever succeed in this calling without any pre-knowledge and experience? How am I even sure that the Lord indeed called me?*" He could have asked for signs to prove the Lord. He also had the option of running away from Elijah, for the fear of the challenges faced by the prophets of God in Israel at that time. Remember that at that time, Ahab and his wicked wife Jezebel were still alive. If a mighty man such as Elijah got frustrated by the wickedness and stubbornness of heart of the Israelites and their king, how then can Elisha survive! Therefore,

Elisha could have thought of all these and run away or refuse the calling.

However, Elisha would not do any of such. He understood clearly what the casting of mantle meant, with joy, therefore, he was ready to serve the Lord. Elisha must have known that men of God have ability to do extra-ordinary things because of the Spirit of God that is upon them. For there is no difference between a great man of God and an unbeliever, except, for the Spirit of the Lord upon that great man of God. Many Christians shy away from responsibilities, they keep complaining about their inability and weakness. Though they are born-again and they frequently quote Philippians 4:13.

"I can do all things through Christ which strengtheneth me"

Despite this, they still believe they are too small or young to accomplish a task committed to them by the Lord. Successful men do not avoid challenges; rather, they face it and overcome. To move into the class of legends, you must stop believing in your strength and weakness. Rather, know that your strength is in the Lord not in yourself. The men of old that achieved greatness in life never achieved that through their power or might. Abraham became the friend of God not because his father was a worshipper of God. In his days, there was no Bible, no scriptures to read about God, yet Abraham walked with the Lord and became the father of faith. But, what made David to overcome Goliath through the use of a stone? Was it not the finger of the Lord? Receiving training in the field or being mentored by a true servant of the Lord will help an upcoming legend to succeed greatly in his calling. Almost every man of God used for mighty works in the Bible days was led by the Lord to acquire some training. God changes not. For the man Moses to acquire administrative ability, God arranged that Moses be taken to the palace of Pharaoh and spent forty years there. Moses acquired personnel training from the palace of the first civilised country. Invariably, Moses got the best personnel training available on earth. Thereafter, God led Moses to the home of Jethro the priest of God for him to acquire spiritual training. God did all these that Moses could make a successful administrator and prophet (Acts 7:22). And Moses has a record in the scriptures that he was a prophet without equal.

Before God could replace Moses, He made Joshua to be tutored by Moses for decades. In fact, when Moses was on the mountain for forty days and forty nights, Joshua too was at the foot of the mountain for the same period. Someone would ask "Brother Oduniyi, how did you know that?" Well, when Moses was coming down from the mountain and Joshua heard the noise of the people he said to Moses;

"…There is a noise of war in the camp"

But Moses said to Joshua; *"It is not the voice of them that shout for mastery, neither is it the voice of them that cry for being overcome: but the noise of them that sing do I hear"* (Exodus 32:17-18).

If Joshua were to be with the people, he would not have misunderstood what the noise meant. In Exodus 33:7-11, we read that there was a Tent of Meeting pitched outside the camp where Moses used to meet with the Lord. Any time the people have something to ask from the Lord, Moses would go into the Tent to inquire from the Lord. And when Moses entered the Tent, the people would rise and stand at the entrances to their own tents and when Moses entered into the Tent of Meeting, pillar of cloud would come down and stay at the entrance of the Tent. Immediately the people saw the pillar of cloud, the people would rise and worship the Lord each at the entrances of their tents. The Lord would speak with Moses face to face, as a man would talk to his friend. Then Moses would return to the camp, but his aide Joshua did not leave the Tent. Joshua chose to remain right in the Tent. He knew at least how God used to speak with Moses. Just as Moses had a direct contact with God, Joshua also had direct contact with God.

"And there arose not a prophet since in Israel like unto Moses, whom the Lord knew face to face" (Deuteronomy 34:10).

Once He has interest in you, God does not need your working experience before He can employ you into His service. All that the Lord wants from you is your total obedience, your readiness to serve Him in all sincerity. Before God chose Elisha, He saw the sons of the prophets that were quite experienced. God will not send a man on a mission without equipping him.

Sometimes, the training period is like a fiery trial. The training period is also a time when God breaks us thoroughly and then remould us. God did it for Moses. In Egypt, he was the apparent heir to the throne. He was to become the next Pharaoh. However, Moses could not talk! In fact, Moses told the Lord when the Lord called him; *"I am not eloquent...I am slow of speech, and of a slow tongue!"* (Exodus 4:10). At the end of his ministry however, the Bible has this testimony about Moses; *"So Moses ...was mighty (powerful) in his speech and in deeds"* (Acts 7:22 AMP). There was a transformation in his life. Imagine the experiences Moses probably had in the midst of other princes. By virtue of his birth, he has more access to the throne, however, here was the apparent heir to the throne of the first civilized nation that had problem with speech. During the first forty years of his life, God broke Moses completely, Moses through that experience learnt humility. Therefore, as he met the Lord, and received both the calling and the anointing, he became a humble man. The word of God has this testimony about Moses, saying that *"Now Moses was a very humble man, more humble than anyone else on the face of the earth"* (Numbers 12:3).

Such is the training of the legend, it is like the word of God in Isaiah 48:10 when the Lord said; *"Behold, I have refined thee, but not with silver; I have chosen thee in the furnace of affliction"* The tribulation, rejection, the pains among others that you may be passing through might have been allowed or permitted by God in other to train you. Absolutely nothing happens in the life of a child of God without a purpose. Consider David, he was hated by his brothers, his father did not consider him to be present along with his other children when Samuel came to chose king among his children. He forgot and locked out David out of his mind. Until Samuel rejected all the children presented before him and asked if Jesse still had some other children, Jesse did not mention anything about David. That was rejection. As part of his training period, David had to fight with a lion and a bear before the Lord allowed Goliath to appear before him. So, training can as well be like passing through the fire, but it is to bring out the best of us. Hence, it is not when the legends manifest that they are made, the training starts far back into their lives. When they manifest is when God reveals them that they might take their rightful place.

Having said that pre-knowledge and past experiences are not necessary, the Lord has a way of training the replacement. After Elisha had been called in 1 Kings 19:19-21 during the reign of King Ahab, Ahab still lived for about three years. The Bible tells us that after three years of peace between Israel and Syria, Ahab went to war with the Syrians and was killed during that war (1 Kings 22). Ahaziah the next king reigned for two years before he died, yet Elijah outlived Ahaziah. King Ahaziah died in II Kings 1. In fact, Elijah predicted the death of Ahaziah. Then in II Kings 2, Elijah was taken to heaven. This simply tells us that for about five years, the Lord delayed the departure of Elijah for one thing, that Elisha might be trained. For during those five years, Elijah was off the stage.

God would not have delayed the departure of Elijah if the training of Elisha was not necessary. Elisha needed to know how a prophet of the Living God should talk, walk, and work. He needed to know how to relate with God, how he should handle every situation facing him in life. He needed to know the purpose of the Lord's anointing upon his life and how to achieve the purpose. There are many so called church leaders and pastors, many Church workers that do not prosper in their ministry because they reject training, they lack knowledge. Many wrongly think that once they got the appointment, automatically, God would set into action as if they have no input to make. Some other Christians are satisfied with the gifts, not knowing that they need to know how to administer properly the gifts in other to profit the body of Christ. Think of the boy Samuel, for some years he had been living with Eli the priest of God. Yet he did not know the voice of God, he could not differentiate between the voice of God and that of a man. The Lord called Samuel the first time, he went to Eli, but Eli said "*I called not, my son*". The second time Samuel heard him being called again, he went again to Eli, Eli told him the same thing.

"And Samuel did not yet know the Lord, neither was the word of the Lord yet revealed unto him" (1 Samuel 3:7).

Despite the fact that Samuel was sleeping in the Temple for years, the word of God says *"And Samuel did not yet know the Lord"* He would open the Temple doors in the morning and shut it at night, yet he did not know the Owner of the Temple he was keeping. Thank-God that after the third call, Eli perceived that Samuel must have been called by the Lord and therefore taught the boy how to respond to the call. Supposing Samuel was not put through by Eli, after several calls, Samuel might miss the opportunity until some other time, and that could be months or years. How many times do we have dreams and as we woke up, we forgot, or lack the interpretations. Unless we do what is demanded to always remember our dreams the situation may not change. Unless we do what is demanded to know the interpretation of the things revealed to us, we may continue to lose the purpose of the Lord and the blessings attached to that purpose.

God's kingdom operates on keys

"And I will give unto thee the keys of the kingdom of heaven" (Matthew 16:19).

The earlier we know that we live in a kingdom that operates on keys the better for us. In our homes, we have different keys; the key that opens the main gate of the house is not the same that opens the main door into the house. Another different key opens your bedroom, and a different one opens your wardrobes. The kingdom of God is operated on keys and the Lord has given us the keys, unless we use the right key, access may prove difficult. Just as a mistake of using a wrong key to open your wardrobe denies you access even though you are the rightful owner. It will not respect you unless you respect the laid down rules, the standard, you will be denied access. The earlier we know the right key to what we need the easier it is for us to have success without stress.

"And a certain Jew named Apollos, born at Alenxandria, an eloquent man, and mighty in the scriptures, came to Ephesus. This man was instructed in the way of the Lord; and being fervent in the

Spirit, he spake and taught diligently the things of the Lord, knowing only the baptism of John" (Acts 18:24-25).

Apollos was a Jew, very eloquent and had a thorough knowledge of the scriptures. He spoke with great fervour and taught about Jesus *accurately*. No doubt, Apollos was anointed and gifted. But, there was something still lacking in his life, he only knew the baptism of John while he knew nothing about the baptism of the Lord which is Holy Ghost baptism. As Priscilla and Aquila listened to Apollos, they discovered what he lacked.

"And he (Apollos) began to speak boldly in the synagogue: whom when Aquila and Priscilla had heard, they took him unto them, and expounded unto him the way of God more perfectly" (Acts18:26).

This couple, Aquila and his wife Priscilla invited Apollos and taught him the way of the Lord more perfectly. Though Apollos had thorough knowledge of the scriptures, and taught about Jesus accurately, when Aquila and Priscilla called him for teaching, into a short training, he never rejected. He humbled himself to be taught, that he might become more useful in the ministry committed to his hand. Thereafter, Apollos went to Achaia, there the Bible told us that he was a great help to the believers there. Then he went to Corinth. This same Apollos now became a man of God some believers in Corinth preferred to Paul and Peter. He that will become great in life must be a good friend of knowledge. We can not wave aside knowledge if we must excel in our calling. Just as God would not personally teach Samuel how to know that it was the Lord calling, since He had blessed him with Eli, so also, God would not step in to teach someone personally if He had blessed that person with someone through whom he can learn. Although the Lord had rejected King Saul as king over Israel and had immediately anointed David still, for over a decade, David did not gain access to the throne. However, he gained access to live in the palace, to eat and dine with the king. David was a shepherd, he had experience in animal rearing, but now he needed to keep people, the people of God. For a shepherd of animal to become shepherd of people, he needed to be trained in that line. Therefore, an access was given to David to live with King

Saul in the palace. There, David acquired skill. Therefore the Psalmist wrote about the reign of David;

"So he fed them according to the integrity of his heart; and guided them by the skilfulness of his hands" (Psalm 78:72).

For Moses, he learnt political training from the palace of king Pharaoh, while he learnt the spiritual from the house of Jethro the priest of God. For a child of God, nothing is accidental; it is arranged by the Lord. For the Apostles of the Lord, they were unschooled, ordinary fishermen. However, they were trained by the Lord Jesus for about three years of His ministry. As if the three years training was not enough, after His resurrection, for forty days, the Lord appeared to His disciples and taught them on things that pertained to the kingdom of God (Acts 1:3).

The man that will come into the class of legends must be eager to learn, a lover of knowledge, and must be teachable. They that assume that they have known it all do not prosper more than the level they were when that evil thought came to their minds. Many are some Christians that feel that they have known the Lord. Yet, we shall continue to know the Lord, every day we live on earth. No one can claim to have known all about Him no matter how great that person can be. The day you assume that you have known all about Him is the day you stop knowing Him.

This is the more reason the Church should organise training programmes for the members on different aspects of life; salvation, the ministry, marriage, finance, and organising formal training (spiritual and otherwise) for the people serving in the Church in different ministry and sections. We can as well read books relevant to our ministry.

It will be wrong to end this chapter without talking about an Apostle of the Lord that we might say he was not mentored by the apostles that knew the Lord before him. That was Apostle Paul. However, before his conversion, he was well schooled and trained by a well respected lawyer in the land of Israel then-Gamaliel. It is therefore not surprising that he wrote more epistles than any other apostle of Jesus in his days. Having said all that, however, he was not taught Christ by any mortal man. You know he was used to learning, studying the Book was not a difficult thing for him at all. Paul did something many Christians do not pay much attention to. Immediately Paul got born-again he went to Arabia. There he was alone with God for three years to learn at the feet of the Lord. Yes, for one thousand and ninety-five days he was alone with God in real study and prayer to know the Lord. And when he came from that three-year training, he rose on the wings like eagles, and he shined more than all other apostles.

Chapter Ten
You are a king by appointment

If only we know who we are and live as such, the devil would have been in greater problem, the kingdom of darkness would have suffered more, the church would have prospered greatly as the gospel is preached throughout the world, then, the Lord would have come. But, the unfortunate thing is that most Christians do not know they are kings by appointment.

"And I appoint unto you a kingdom, as my Father hath appointed unto me" (Luke 22:29).

Just as the Father appointed to Jesus a kingdom, Jesus too appointed to us a kingdom. Not just that.

"And hast made us unto our God kings and priests: and we shall reign on the earth" (Revelations 5:10).

There is no king without a kingdom, so also there is no kingdom without a king. The Lord has appointed to us a kingdom, and has made us kings and priests to our God. The above scriptural verses are meant for all that believe and accept Jesus as their Lord and Saviour. God has no grand-children therefore the Bible says we are co-heirs with Christ Jesus. God has given all His children equal opportunity. Hence, Jesus promised that we shall do all that He did, and even greater works we shall do. Every child of God has equal right before God. However, our success now depends on how much we make good use of these rights. Our Father gives us equal access to His riches, how wealthy we are depends on how much we draw from His riches. All that the Lord did during His earthly ministry He did as a king and a priest.

"Where the word of a king is, there is power: and who may say unto him, What doest thou?" (Ecclesiastes 8:4).

"How God anointed Jesus of Nazareth with the Holy Ghost and with power: who went about doing good, and healing all that were oppressed of the devil, for God was with Him" (Acts 10:38).

The Lord lived the life of a king, He feared no evil. He lived a victorious life. He was a great threat to the devil and to all demons. He went about seeking for the people that the devil had held captives, as He found them, He set them free, and the devil had nothing to say or do against Jesus. For where the word of a king is, there is power and nobody can question his authority. Everything that happened to Jesus and around Him happened to bring glory to God. When His disciples lacked enough bread in the wilderness, yet He had thousands of people to feed, inadequate food became surplus food. In fact, the left-over was more than the initial food that was blessed. At the wedding at Cana, when wine finished, water was turned to good quality wine. On the sea, when the wind was blowing against His ship, He was not bothered. He just slept, for He knew it was impossible for the sea to swallow Him. When the faithless disciples woke Him up, He just spoke the word, the word of a king, and just immediately, the wind ceased. At another time, when He knew that the wind was tormenting His disciples on the sea, and there was no ship to take Him, He stepped on the water and the water could not swallow Him, He walked on and on, right on the water. When He got to His disciples, without saying any word concerning the storm and the wind, as He stepped into the ship, the storm and the wind just ceased. Jesus was a blessing to people wherever He went. He had a power of a king and demonstrated that power. Where the word of a king is, there is power. To raise the dead girl of Jarius, He just said;

"Damsel, I say unto thee, arise. And straightway the damsel arose, and walked; for she was the age of twelve years" (Mark 5:41-42).

When Lazarus was dead, and Jesus got there, He also said the word of a king, therefore death could not say "What are you doing to my captive?" Jesus did not even recognise death, He just said;

"Lazarus, come forth. And he that was dead came forth" (John 11:43-44).

All that Jesus needed to perform miracles was to say the word.

"Where the word of a king is, there is power: and who may say unto him, What doest thou?" (Ecclesiastes 8:4).

Jesus was and is still a King, during His ministry He lived as King, and now too, He still exercises the power of a King, even of the King of kings. He has promised that we shall do more than He did. But some lack this knowledge.

"Therefore my people are gone into captivity, because they have no knowledge: and their honourable men are famished, and their multitude dried up with thirst" (Isaiah 5:13).

People that are anointed and appointed to cast out demons are being oppressed, suppressed and tormented by demons. Yet the Lord had said;

"In my name shall they cast out devils..." (Mark 16:17).

Despite this, the devil keeps destroying their marriages, education, businesses and their ministry. Yet, they that know their God shall be strong and do exploit. But for those that do not know their God, they shall be exploited. Our inability and failure to exploit will make us to be exploited. Only the strong can exploit, the weak are exploited. Of course you know that babes are weak. But, you are a king, a king by appointment. You are appointed as king by the King of kings. You are a king, do not live as a slave. Rise up to live as a king. Reject the life of a slave. We are anointed to cast out and displace demons. Our manifestation alone is powerful to destroy the works of the devil. This is the right and the position of every Christian. I think it is a shameful thing when demons begin to harass and push Christians around. The king has the final say in his kingdom, the final word rests with the king. We have the final word on every issue that affects us. No devil or demon has the final say about any aspect of your life, you have the final say.

A born legend

Every Christian is a born legend. We are not born to be ordinary, rather we are born great. When you became born-again, God gave birth to you through His word that you might be famous, and when He gave you His Holy Spirit, He gave that so that you might be outstandingly good in the ministry He has committed into your hand. God did not give us His Holy Spirit that we might speak in tongue alone, He gave us His Spirit that we might be legends in this world. We are born to rule. We are born kings! As Christians, we are supposed to be solution carriers, for we are Holy Ghost carriers. When we come in contact with people that have problems, our presence should usher in solution to their problems. The men of the town of Jericho told Elisha that the town was well situated, but the water was bad and the land was unproductive. Elisha did not search long for solution, the day he was told of the problem of the town, the same day the water was healed and the land became productive (2 Kings 2:19-22).

Apostle Peter was called upon to attend to Dorcas, a woman reported to be full of good works. They sent for Peter for they knew his coming would bring solution to the problem at hand. Peter was a legend. However, ignorance, laziness or lack of interest to be great has kept many Christians to remain ordinary therefore they rely on the legend for survival. Peter went there, and Dorcas lived again.

"Blessed be the God and the Father of our Lord Jesus Christ, who hath blessed us with all spiritual blessings in heavenly places in Christ" (Ephesians 1:3).

God did not bless some of us, rather, He has blessed us, all of us with all the spiritual blessings that ever exist in the heavenly places. We all have been blessed, not with few or many blessings but with all blessings that our Father has in heavens. What do you intend to do with these blessings? It is high time we stopped living wretched spiritual life, for we have been blessed with all spiritual blessings in the heavenly places. The Lord knows that a king needs resources in other to remain powerful in his kingdom, hence He has blessed us. You are an appointed king, appointed to rule the world through your word. As a king, you are appointed to be fruitful, to multiply, replenish, subdue and dominate. Do not fail to manifest any of these five features of a king. Jesus as well as the men of old lived as kings. You are not inferior unless you make yourself inferior.

"And hast made us unto our God kings and priests: and we shall reign on earth" (Revelation 5:10).

In this kingdom that is appointed to us, no one can be a king without being a priest. A priest is an anointed man of God, appointed to offer sacrifices and prayers to God for the people. The priest goes to God to intercede for the people. As he prays for the people, he offers sacrifices to God on their behalf. A priest is a friend of God, always in the presence of God. Jesus gave us an example of the life of a priest. After performing many miracles, He would send the people away, He would despatch His disciples also, while He alone would go up to the mountain to pray. In most cases, He did it more when He had had a busy day. At a time when we would have assumed that He must be too tired to be alone with God, even then He would pray from night till daybreak. It was during such a time that Elijah and Moses appeared to Him on the mountain. He therefore counselled us;

"Men ought always to pray, and not faint" (Luke 18:1).

Jesus did not for once allow His work to reduce the time He spent in His personal devotion. Even when He had a busy day, He would spend the night with the Father. His frequent appearances before the Father was to glorify the Father, to acknowledge His support and faithfulness, to renew His strength and commit His next assignment to the Father. He was never too busy to spend enough time with the Father in His personal prayer. The pressure of His work would not reduce the time He would spend with the Father. As a result, the Father kept backing Him up.

The work of a priest is in the presence of our heavenly Father. As priests, we live sanctified life that we may be able to offer acceptable sacrifices to God. As priests, in our closet we worship and exalt Him, we intercede for the people and ask for His favour as we go out to manifest as kings.

However, the duty of a king is performed outside, among the people, exercising God-given authority over sicknesses, demons and the devil. We are both kings and priests. Failure to be a committed priest, makes one a weakling and ineffective king. A successful priest before the Father is a powerful king before men and the kingdom of darkness.

Many people have more desire to manifest as kings than to perform their duties as priests. Just as our sitting determines our rising, our kneels determine our power, the efficacy of our word. If on your kneels, you are strong before the Father, your rising before men will be in glory and power.

The Lord is still searching for more legends, mighty people to be raised in His army. Many legends are preparing to go. Vacuum will not be created therefore God needs replacement for them. God anointed two kings and a prophet to replace Elijah, only God knows the number of people He needs for each of the legends we have around us today. You have an opportunity to become a legend of the King of kings, do not throw away this opportunity. God has given you the grace to become an important soldier in His army, do not frustrate this grace. Arise today to enable your light shine.

The highly exalted ones

"Then thou spakest in vision to thy holy one, and saidst, I have laid help upon one that is mighty; I have exalted one chosen out of the people" (Psalm 89:19).

The Lord causes His sun to rise on the good and evil, and sends rain on both the righteous and the unrighteous. There are some blessings of the Lord that are general, you do not need to be godly before you can access and enjoy them. However, there are some blessings of God that are reserved only for His own people. To access and enjoy such blessings, you must fulfil the terms of the covenant. And, whenever God begins to demarcate or differentiate who and who should enjoy His blessings, you can be sure that great blessings, mighty miracles are involved.

At the Kebar river, Ezekiel along with other exiles from Jerusalem were there, but, only Ezekiel saw the heavens opened and saw the visions of God that ended up in bringing him out of great multitudes, gave him a great name, such that, when all the people in his generation had all died, Ezekiel still lives on. He is alive in the word of God and he's read everyday in many nations by people of different races.

When God began to deal harshly with the Egyptians because of Pharaoh's refusal to let the Israelites go, God began to demarcate between the Israelites and the Egyptians. For three days, there was such a thick darkness that could be felt, but only in the land where the Egyptians dwelt, while the Israelites had light at Goshen. When the destroying angel was set to go and kill the entire first born of both men and animals in Egypt, God caused a demarcation. As a result, while there were great death, weeping and sorrow among the Egyptians, the Israelites had joy and deliverance.

At a time when there was a great famine in the land of the Philistines, while the Philistines sowed, Isaac the son of Abraham the friend of God also sowed. However, the seed sown by the Philistines were destroyed by the great famine. It was a great natural disaster. Though Isaac was in the same land, somehow by the hand of God, Isaac reaped such a great bountiful harvest that made him to become wealthier than the whole nation of the Philistines, and that miraculous wealth got during a great famine made the Philistines to envy Isaac.

This practice of the Lord is not limited to the Old Testament days, just as God changes not, His word also changes not, and His deeds too never change. Consider Saul that later became Paul the apostle.

On his way to Damascus, he was not alone in the mission to arrest and imprison Christians in that region. However, he alone saw the vision that later changed his life. He alone among all the people that went on that journey is known today and he alone became great.

Each time God speaks to specific person or a group of people while others are kept away, God surely means business and aims at something great. That is why it is important you pay attention to what the Lord is saying to you, more especially if it looks as if you are the only one that sees it differently. Go to God to have the full knowledge of what the Lord is saying to you, just as Paul went to the land of Arabia to confirm and understand fully the meaning of the vision the Lord showed him on his way to Damascus.

"Then thou spakest in vision to thy holy people..." (Psalm 89:19)

The New International Version puts it this way; *"Once you spoke in a vision, to your faithful people you said..."*

God focused His attention on His holy one, the faithful people in the sight of God. Now, God is not talking to everyone. He is not talking to sinners who are yet to repent. He is not talking to the backsliders who are still contemplating whether to come back to the Lord or still stay away for a while. God is into a serious talk with His faithful ones, people that have given their lives to Jesus no matter what may befall them. They are people that will not steal because they lack money and yet hungry; people that will not be involved in illicit business due to lack of job; people that have decided not to lie even when their lives are at stake. God is talking to such people.

"...I have bestowed strength on a warrior..." (Psalm 89:19 NIV).

If you are not ready to join the army of a nation, you cannot expect the government of that nation to supply you with guns and ammunitions. If a nation will entrust into your hand authority to use ammunitions and weapons, then you must enrol in the army. It is the same with God. God bestows strength on a warrior. A Christian that hates going into spiritual battles is really not ready to fulfil his destiny in Christ. The Lord made this clear saying;

"...Now the kingdom of heaven suffereth violence, and the violent take it by force" (Matthew 11:12).

142

A Christian that fears isn't ready to possess his possession. It is important to know this: to access the Promised-land, there are two ways. To fulfil your destiny (as a born-again Christian) there are two ways set before you. The position of your heart will determine which way the Lord will lead you through.

*"And it came to pass, when Pharaoh had let the people go, that God led them not through the way of the land of the Philistines, although **that was near**; for God said, Lest peradventure the people repent when they see war, and they return to Egypt. But God led the people about, through the way of the wilderness of the Red sea..."* (Exodus 13:17-18).

It was not part of God's original plan to lead the Israelites through the way of the wilderness. God had no intention to make His people to have the wilderness experience they went through at that time. God also did not have any intention to have His people spent forty years before they would reach the promised-land. God knew the short way to the promised-land, but the people were fearful. If however God chose not to let the people go through the way of the wilderness, the only option open is to let the people reach the promised-land quickly, so fast. However, since giants are there in the promised-land to resist and fight against the Israelites, God knew what the Israelites would do, since they were fearful, they would not mind to return to Egypt, the land of slavery. The truth is, if they returned to Egypt, they would die in Egypt without any deliverance. The same thing happens these days. Supposing God gave you a better job, even though at your former place of work your employer was begging you not to go, in fact he was ready to increase your salary, if that would make you stay. But, because this new job has more prospects, you decided to take up the new job. Supposing after resumption on the new job great persecutions of various forms and from different colleagues came against you. Wouldn't you consider going back to your former job? That is what a fearful man would do. Rather than taking up the challenge in the name of the Lord, searching through the Scriptures to discover what the Lord has said concerning the situation, such a fearful man would sit down and begin to regret ever leaving his former job. To avoid that therefore, if a man is afraid of the giants, of great challenges, God will permit that such a man be led through the way of the wilderness.

The truth of the matter is this: no matter the way you pass through, you cannot escape facing the giants on the way to success and breakthrough. You see, when God led the Israelites out of Egypt (which was the land of slavery) God was determined to lead them all to the promised-land. God had earlier promised Abraham that at a particular year, He would rescue Abraham's children from the land of slavery. God was committed to fulfil His word. Nothing would make God fail to take the Israelites out of Egypt at that time. Since God could not deny His word, He took them out of Egypt.

Think of all that the children of Israel went through in the wilderness. As they had the miracle of crossing the Red sea and were rejoicing, there came suddenly the problem of lack of drinkable water. For about three days the whole multitude had no water to drink. Suddenly again, they saw water from afar, they all rushed to it, only to find out that the water was bitter. Then they became angry with both Moses and the Lord. Thereafter, the waters at Marah were healed. From the very day they crossed the Red sea to when the Israelites got to the promised-land, they kept moving from one tribulation to another. They had no lasting peace, all the generations that left Egypt died at the wilderness, including Moses, Aaron and Miriam-the prophetess. You see, the members of the Church that are prone to fear can, if care is not taken, make their pastors miss the kingdom of heaven. The reason is that the pastors may become worried when they see their members moving from one tribulation to another, when they face destruction from both the enemy and from the Lord. It was through such events in the wilderness that made Moses, Aaron and Miriam fall in the wilderness. They all died where the fearful died. In fact, the Bible kept the death of Miriam off record. At the end of the day, the children of these fearful people still faced, fought against and conquered the giants that made their fathers went through the terrible wilderness experience.

The fact that you meet the giants, who may appear as great

challenges and difficulties, great tribulation and persecution, simply shows that you have reached the gate or border of the promised-land. Why? Because the giants are not really on the way, they are in the promised-land. The twelve Israeli spies sent to go and survey Canaan saw the giants living in the Promised-land, not on the way. The rich do not live along in the road, they dwell in mansions. Hence, whenever you encounter the giants, it is an indication that you are already in the Promised-land, therefore, do not be scared by them. All that the giants want to do is to scare you. They know quite well that if they engage you in warfare they cannot overcome, but once they can just succeed in instilling fear in you, then they can win. Do not buy that lie. Stay put!

Do not be afraid of any challenges. Once the Lord is with you, you belong to a winning team. In a winning team there is no loser, everyone is a winner. Whatever your visions are, do not compromise. Go ahead, press forward at the goal. Do not be bothered on how to get certain things needed to achieve the goal. God is greater than the resources you need to succeed. The Giver of the vision is also the Giver of the resources needed to accomplish the vision. Your Partner in the journey is a specialist in converting impossibilities into possibilities. If He wants to shame the rich on how to get money, God may instruct a fish to produce money from its mouth for the servant of the Lord. God is never held in a tight corner. That is why He is Almighty God, the Possessor of heaven and the earth. He can do and undo. No one can question Him.

Once you are not afraid of the giants, God is ready to bestow strength on you. Now, if God gives you strength, then with whose strength are you fighting? The strength of God! Since no one can overcome God, it means as you receive and fight with the strength of God, no one and no situation can overcome you. Take note of this: each time you fear, it means you trust in your own human power. But when you trust on the strength on the Lord, you will fear no fear.

The word of the Lord in Psalm 89:19-27 reads;

"Once you spoke in a vision, to your faithful people you said: "I have bestowed strength on a warrior; I have exalted a young man

from among the people. I have found David my servant; with my sacred oil I have anointed him. My hand will sustain him; surely my arm will strengthen him. No enemy will subject him to tribute; no wicked man will oppress him. I will crush his foes before him and strike down his adversaries. My faithful love will be with him, and through my name his horn will be exalted. I will set his hand over the rivers. He will call out to me, 'You are my Father, my God, the Rock my Saviour'. I will also appoint him my firstborn, the most exalted of the kings of the earth" (NIV).

In the above scripture, God only exalted David and we can see all that he enjoyed simply because God exalted him. It is important that you understand this aspect of this book for you to really have the worth for the money paid to purchase the book and the time spent reading the book. If on the table you have cups of water and you lift up a cup, what will happen? The cup lifted up becomes unique among its mates. It is seen more than others. It enjoys air at a temperature different from other cups. And it is above other cups! When God exalted David, David received God's anointing. Even though Jesse the father of David had neglected David for not considering him as one worth being anointed as king, God spoke clearly to Samuel that the king was not among the children of Jesse presented before Samuel. Until Samuel questioned Jesse if he had another son, Jesse did not say he had another. Since God had exalted David, nobody could hide or put him away on the day of honour. No devil or human judgement could rob him of God's blessing. For when Samuel saw the first born of Jesse, he quickly assumed that he was the one God wanted to anoint. He judged by what he saw. But God quickly cautioned Samuel that he was wrong. When God exalts you, nothing under the heaven can hide you from being blessed. God's glory upon your life cannot be hidden by anything. It will show. Why? The Lord has placed His glory above the heavens, where no devil can reach. His glory is placed above all, nothing can cover it!

When David was exalted, the lion and the bear couldn't kill him. Though he was a boy, under eighteen year-old, a lion was too weak to kill him, simply because God had exalted him. God exalted David to be above the type of people that could be devoured by animals. Dear friend, are you exalted by the Lord? If you say yes, how do you know this? What prove do you have from the word of the Lord? If you are exalted, you will enjoy what David enjoyed. But you must know it and see it before you can begin to enjoy the benefits of those exalted by the Lord. Even though Goliath was a giant, all the warriors in Israel feared him including Saul the king. Each time Goliath came out to defile the armies of Israel, there would be a great silence in the camp of the Israelites. Although David was a shepherd without any experience in war fare, and Goliath was a giant and a champion, Goliath was too weak to stand before David. With all his armour, and war experience, he was too weak to remain on his feet before David. It was not because David was brave, but because God was fighting the battle. David was just a figure head in battle. You can read the testimony of David in the II Samuel 22:1;

"And David spake unto the Lord the words of this song in the day that the Lord had delivered him out of the hand of all his enemies, and out of the hand of Saul."

David sat before the Lord and began to express his gratitude in song. In verse 18 he said

"He delivered me from my strong enemy, and from them that hated me: for they were too strong for me."

So, there were some enemies that were too strong for David to confront. If not for God they would have killed him. In verse 30 he said this;

"For by thee I have run through a troop: by my God have I leaped over a wall"

David ran through a battalion of soldiers of an enemy nation yet he was not hurt. What gave him such protection? You can see this in verse 36;

"You give me your shield of victory; you stoop down to make me great"

God's own shield of victory, shield of salvation that protects God from harm was given to David. Just meditate on this for awhile.

David received God's shield of victory, how then could he have suffered defeat! No wonder he kept escaping from harm and destruction, for God had given him divine shield of victory. That is the shield that ensures victory no matter what. That is the portion of the man that is exalted by the Lord. Let me ask you a question here; choose one out of these three questions: Are you exalted, or you will pray so that the Lord may exalt you or, are you highly exalted already? I am asking you these questions because our faith determines how far and how much we can enjoy in Christianity. David said that God stoop down to make him great. King James Version said it this way;

"Thy gentleness made me great"

When you are exalted, through the gentleness of the Lord, you will become great. In verse 40, David confirmed the word of the Lord in Psalm 89 by saying;

"You armed me with strength for battle; you made my adversaries bow at my feet. You made my enemies turn their backs in flight, and I destroyed my foes"

Yes, some of the enemies of David could pray, and in fact they did pray to the Lord, but the Lord refused to answer them (verse 41) That simply means, God is not going to answer the prayer of your enemies that may want to harm you. When you are competing for a position with other people who claim to also know this same God, once you fall into the class of the exalted ones, which of course is the class of the legends, let them pray, God will rather give them another blessing. Any prayer that will hurt you will not be heard by God. In verses 44 and 45, David revealed that it was God that made his enemies to loose heart, they became trembling and so, they surrendered to David, saying, *"we will serve you, only let us live"*. And on the victories that David had, how did he have them, was it by his strength and military training? Let us read the testimony of David;

"He gives His king great victories; He shows unfailing kindness to His anointed, to David and his descendants for ever."

David had all the victories as gifts from God. God gave him

victories as a father will give his son gift. The life of King David revealed the life of someone that is exalted by God. He was the only king in Israel that was exalted by God. Therefore, he was the only king in Israel that was both a king and a prophet. Thus, he had both the anointing of a king and that of a prophet. He was above his contemporaries in all ways. Yes, of all the kings that reigned in Israel, including Solomon that was the wisest man that ever lived on earth aside Jesus, only David was the man after God's heart. If David that was exalted enjoyed all these privileges, what do you think the portion of the man that is **highly** exalted will be? May I ask you these questions again; are you exalted, or you will pray to God to exalt you, or are you highly exalted already?

Let me say here that, once you are born-again, you do not need to pray before you will be exalted, and the truth is that you are not just exalted, rather, you are highly exalted! You are not going to be highly exalted rather, you are already highly exalted. Prayer is not going to take you to the place, rather faith through the knowledge of what the Lord has done for you will take you there. Let us read this about Jesus;

"Wherefore God also hath highly exalted Him, and given Him a name which is above every name: that at the name of Jesus every knee should bow, of things in heaven, and things in earth, and things under earth; and that every tongue should confess that Jesus Christ is Lord, to the glory of God the Father" (Philippians 2:9-11).

God did not just exalt Jesus. For Jesus was not to belong to the class of David. In the book of Psalm, when David was speaking through the Holy Spirit he called Jesus his Lord. If Jesus was the Lord over David, then where is the sign of His lordship if Jesus and David were to belong to the same class? Hence, while David was exalted, Jesus was highly exalted. Of course we can see in the life of Jesus that Jesus was greater than David. While only the knees on earth bowed before David, all knees in heaven, on earth and under the earth bow before mighty Jesus.

Like I once said, once you are born-again you are already highly exalted by God. Now, once you can see it from the scriptures, and the

Holy Spirit helps you to understand this, your manifestation will begin to be like the one that is highly exalted. We were highly exalted during the resurrection of Christ Jesus. By destiny in Christ through redemption, as Jesus was being raised from the dead, the Bible has this record;

"And hath raised us up together, and made us sit together in heavenly places in Christ Jesus" (Ephesians 2:6).

As God was exalting Jesus, we were in Him. So God exalted us together with Jesus. We are made seated in heavenly places on the inside of Jesus Christ. We are in Christ. When a cup of water is lifted up, is it only the cup that is lifted up? Certainly not. As the cup is lifted up, the water inside is also lifted up. If the cup is highly exalted, the water on the inside is also highly exalted. Before you gave your life to Jesus, you were living your life under many things. Different things ruled over you. That is why a natural man will say he is under a circumstance. He is ruled by circumstances. Before you were born-again, the principalities, powers and dominion could exercise their power over you. Sickness could molest you. Demons of failure could threaten. But the day you become born-again, your position in life changes. You are no longer permitted to say things like "Well, under that circumstances, I could not ..." Or things like; "I was under pressure" No, you are not under anything; rather all things are under you. I think Christians ought not to speak as the people of the world speak. They speak failure and impossibilities, but since those things are not our portions, we need not speak like them rather we should speak what the word reveals as our portions. Would you ever imagine God saying "Well, under that circumstance, I had to..." Never! God chooses His word, so must we choose our word too. For he that is born-again is born of God. God gives you a new nature, a divine nature from above, hidden in Christ.

"Therefore if any man be in Christ, he is a new creature: old things are passed away; behold, all things are become new" (2 Corinthians 5:17).

"For ye are dead, and your life is hid with Christ in God" (Colossians 3:3).

"He that cometh from above is above all; he that is of the earth is earthly, and speaketh of the earth: he that cometh from heaven is above all" (John 3:31).

Once you know that you are in Christ Jesus the Highly Exalted King, anytime you sing or hear people singing song as this to the Lord;

"You are highly exalted,
There is no one like You,
Halle, halle, halle, hallelujah"

You should see yourself in Christ Jesus, the Highly Exalted King of kings and enjoy your lots as one highly exalted in Christ.

Finally friends, consider the word of the Lord to father Abraham.

"And I will make thee exceeding fruitful, and I will make nations of thee, and kings shall come of thee" (Genesis 17:6).

If you are a child of Abraham you need to know that nations and kings are made out of Abraham, there is no place for servants and slaves. Even Ishmael who was born out of the will of God, born after the flesh still partook of Abraham's blessing. Since he came out of the loins of Abraham he was still a great man. Ishmael gave birth to twelve kings. God specifically told Abraham that He would bless Ishmael because he was a child of Abraham. You can see the wealth of Ishmael from the resources the Arab nations have these days. That was Ishmael a rejected son of Abraham, the one God said Abraham should drive out, child of a slave woman. If he could still enjoy such a great blessing and honour from God simply because he was connected to Abraham, how much more you that is a son of Abraham through the Son of God!

So also Jesus has made us kings and priests to our God, there is no room in Christ for us to be nobody, but important personalities. You are indeed a potential legend of the Lord. Rise up to occupy your position in the Lord. Jesus is highly exalted, you are in Him, you enjoy that privileges that the highly exalted king enjoys. Jesus has made you a priest and a king to our God. You are a king, but not an ordinary king. Just as King David was not an ordinary king among all kings in Israel and on earth, by redemption, you are not an ordinary king. You are a highly exalted king because you live within a better covenant than the Old Covenant during which David lived. You can enjoy abundant life full of promotion and victory. You can be the head and not the tail. You can be above only as God has promised you in the scriptures. No destroyer of destiny is capable of stopping you, for you are not on the same level with them. The circumstances surrounding your birth and your family status and background are too insignificant to hinder you from getting to the top. You have an open cheque placed in your hand to be great in life, to be a legend, a general in the army of the Lord. What you do with this opportunity will determine where you end your journey. Elisha made good use of the opportunity, would you do the same? If you are determined to come out of the crowd, and you are ready to take the bold steps that will launch you into the class of legends, then I say this to you; "See you at the top, in the class of the Legends very soon!"

Jesus is Lord!